Improving Your Project Management Skills

Larry Richman, PMP

American Management Association
New York • Atlanta • Brussels • Chicago • Mexico City • San Francisco
Shanghai • Tokyo • Toronto • Washington, D.C.

*Special discounts on bulk quantities of AMACOM books are available to corporations, professional associations, and other organizations. For details, contact Special Sales Department, AMACOM, a division of American Management Association, 1601 Broadway, New York, NY 10019.
Tel.: 212-903-8316. Fax: 212-903-8083.
Website: www.amacombooks.org*

Library of Congress Cataloging-in-Publication Data

Richman, Larry.
Improving your project management skills / Larry Richman.
p. cm.
Includes bibliographical references and index.
ISBN 0-8144-0875-3 (pbk.)
1. Project management. I. Title.
HD69.P75R526 2006
658.4'04—dc22

2005020268

Printing number

10 9 8 7 6 5 4 3 2 1

Improving Your Project Management Skills

This book is based on the seminar Improving Your Project Management Skills that was developed by Stephen Gershenson, Gershenson & Associates, Inc.; Stuart Syme, Neidpath Solutions Group Inc.; and Michael Bender, Ally Business Developers.

Contents

List of Figures

PART I

FOUNDATIONS FOR SUCCESS

CHAPTER

–1–

The Core Concepts

Projects are an essential part of human history. Some projects arise in myth, some in wartime, some from faith, and others from science and commerce. Some projects are monumental, and others are more modest. Ancient Egypt created the Great Pyramids, the Sphinx, the Library, and the Lighthouse of Alexandria. China's Great Wall, which still stands today, took over 1,000 years to build. Peru's Incan culture left us the lingering splendor of Machu Picchu. In our own time, we have placed men on the moon and returned them safely. We have developed drugs that target specific diseases. We have responded to environmental incidents, managed failures at nuclear sites, and responded to natural disasters. We have linked individuals and organizations through the miracle of the Internet. We have fulfilled the promise of integrated business systems that embrace enterprise resource planning, inventory management, production and control, human resources, and financial systems. This history of accomplishment will not end.

Some projects are ambitious and far-reaching in their social, economic, and political impacts. Others are less grand and more self-contained. Some require advances in basic science, and others deploy proven technology or best practices. Some projects challenge deeply held beliefs, and others uphold traditional values. And some projects fail.

Regardless of time, place, or culture, the dominant characteristic of a project is that it is a goal to be met within the triple expectations (or constraints) of time, cost, and scope. The goal is always to achieve some beneficial change. Every project is an endeavor. Every project is an investment. Every project will end. Some will end when the goal is achieved, and others when the time or cost is disproportionate to the value. Some projects will be cancelled.

In all cases, the project manager serves as the focal point of responsibility for the project's time, cost, and scope. Success requires that the project manager serve as the focal point of effective, timely, and accurate communication. To do this well, the project manager must master a new vocabulary and must use this vocabulary consistently. Words are vehicles of meaning. Consistent use of a common vocabulary is essential to successful communication and, therefore, successful projects.

The aim of this chapter is to help you acquire and use project management vocabulary. It will help you become more familiar with terminology, the need for project management, the six functions of management, *A Guide to the Project Management Body of Knowledge (PMBOK® Guide)*, generic life-cycle processes, and the nine knowledge areas of project management.

Project Management Vocabulary

Effective project management requires a consistent vocabulary, applied consistently. Many project management books try to define key terms with accuracy and precision. This is both fruitful and frustrating. It is fruitful because a common set of terms and concepts improves communication and speeds our work along with minimal confusion. It is occasionally frustrating because important terms have subtlety and nuance associated with them; complex ideas do not have simple essences.

Nonetheless, a core set of ideas, terms, and definitions is helpful. We can establish, by consensus and convention, that words have fairly narrow meanings, that they will be used in certain ways, and that they will be applied consistently throughout this book. The definitions introduced in this chapter are the project manager's methods of art—words and terms used in the context of planning, scheduling, and controlling projects.

"A *project* is a temporary endeavor undertaken to create a unique product, service or result" (*PMBOK® Guide*, third edition, 5). More pointedly, a project is a one-of-a-kind undertaking designed to meet predefined technical and performance targets within the constraints of time and cost. An easy way to view a project is depicted in the project triangle in Figure 1-1.

Figure 1-1. The Project Triangle.

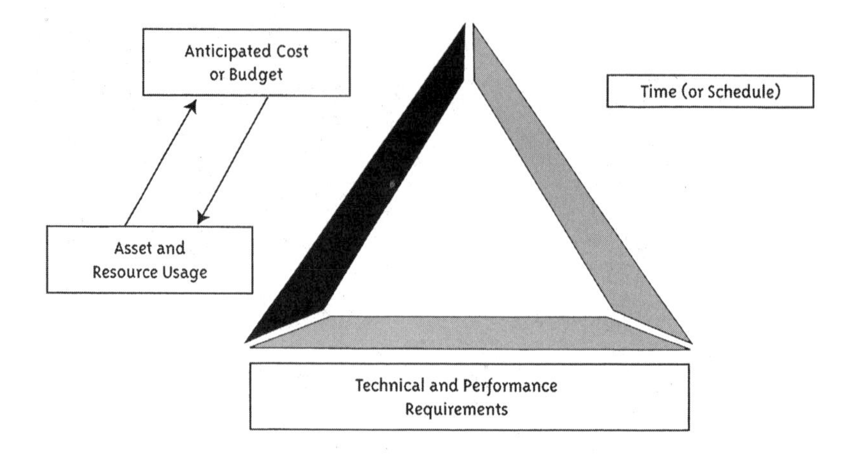

The net result is that projects should be seen as if they were investments. That is, they should produce beneficial results within predefined targets of time, cost, and asset and resource utilization. Under this notion, the project manager is both a change agent and business manager, not merely a technical supervisor.

The benefits may be defined in a variety of ways. One way is to justify a project on the grounds that it ensures an organization's *survival*. Here, the project is mandatory rather than discretionary. It must be done either to comply with government or industry standards, or to sustain operational readiness—for example, repair a leaking roof or an essential manufacturing tool.

Other projects might contribute to improved *profitability*. Projects in this group may provide improved cost controls, margin management, business-process reengineering, system upgrades, streamlined work flows, and strengthened customer satisfaction through product and service improvements. Projects in this area could also include product launches or advertising campaigns, trade show exhibits, packaging changes, office relocations, and organization restructuring.

Finally, there are some projects that try to secure the long-term *growth* of the organization. These strategic projects may seek to extend plant capacity, deploy new or emerging technologies, or bring new products and services to market. Regardless of the underlying reason, every project takes on the appearance of an investment—the need to produce significant benefits within the constraints of time, cost, and asset and resource utilization. Strategic projects, by definition, try to leverage investments so that short-term dollars yield longer-term revenue and profit dollars.

The key is this: Every project must be aligned with something bigger than itself. Each project should be linked to some enterprise goal, objective, or strategy.

The time constraint is defined as the project's *late finish* date. The ceiling on expenditures is the *project budget*. The budget itself is a scorekeeping tool that measures the anticipated rate and timing of expenditures for the labor costs, equipment, material, travel, and other items needed to meet project objectives.

When we link the preceding themes we have *project management*, which is "the application of knowledge, skills, tools and techniques to project activities to meet project requirements" (*PMBOK® Guide*, third edition, 8). The management part involves the acquisition and use of limited resources to meet technical and performance requirements—the project mission. On the other hand, a *program* may involve ongoing work and is understood to be "a group of related projects managed in a coordinated way to obtain benefits and control not available from managing them individually" (*PMBOK® Guide*, third edition, 16).

Increasingly popular today is the notion of *portfolio management*. A portfolio is ''a collection of projects or programs and other work that are grouped together to facilitate effective management of that work to meet strategic business objectives'' (*PMBOK® Guide*, third edition, 16).

Why Project Management?

Project management stems from the need to plan and coordinate large, complex, multifunctional efforts. History provides us with many project examples. We are familiar with Noah's project. The goal was straightforward—build an ark. The material requirements indicated that the ark should be built with gopherwood and to prescribed dimensions. Ulysses built the Trojan Horse. Medieval cathedrals were designed and built over the course of centuries. However, not one of these projects deployed a consistent, coherent methodology of management techniques aimed at schedule development, cost control, resource acquisition and deployment, and risk management.

Project management, as we have come to know it, was the solution to a practical problem. Governmental communications in the latter part of the twentieth century, unfortunately, often involved technical staff speaking only with their technical counterparts in defense-contractor organizations. Each discipline conferred with its own colleagues. Changes in one aspect of a system—say, payload weight—were not always communicated to other interested and affected parties, such as avionics or engine design. Too often, the results were cost and schedule overruns, as well as systems that failed to meet expectations.

The concept emerged of the project manager as a focal point of integration for time, cost, and product quality (see Figure 1-2). This need for a central point of integration was also apparent in many other types of projects. Architectural, engineering, and construction projects were a logical place to use project management techniques. Information systems design and development efforts also were likely candidates to benefit from project management. For projects addressing basic or pure research, principal investigators were no longer only the best scientists, but were also expected to manage the undertaking to one degree or another.

If project management is indeed a solution, then we have to recognize how it reacts and adapts to workplace and marketplace needs such as the following:

- ❑ Higher-quality products
- ❑ More customized products

Figure 1-2. Evolution of Project Management.

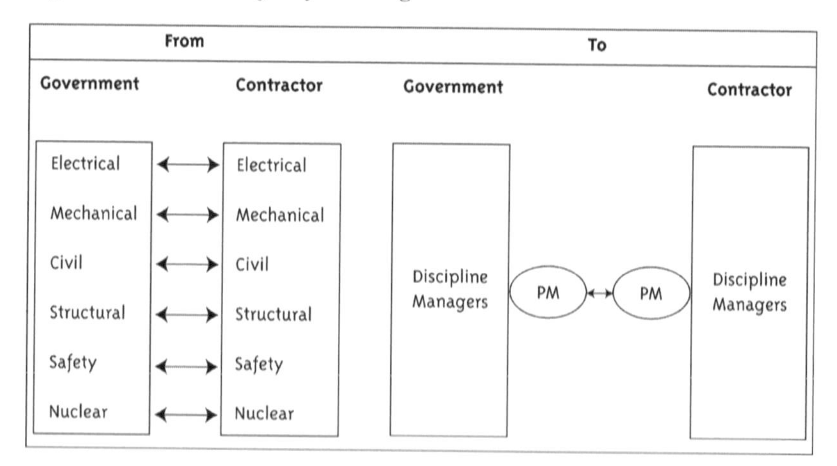

- ❑ Shorter time-to-market
- ❑ Global competition
- ❑ Easier information access
- ❑ Technology growth
- ❑ Global organizations seeking uniform practices

Classic Functions of Management

Management is routinely understood to be accomplishing work through the expenditure of resources. More rigorously, management is the science of employing resources efficiently in the accomplishment of a goal. The classic functions of management are planning, directing, organizing, staffing, controlling, and coordinating.

Planning

Planning is a process. It begins with an understanding of the current situation—the "as-is" state. It goes on to establish a desired future—the "to-be" state. The gap between these two states causes the project manager to identify and evaluate alternative approaches, recommend a preferred course of action, and then synthesize that course of action into a viable plan. Planning raises and answers the questions shown in Figure 1-3.

Directing

Directing communicates the goals, purposes, procedures, and means to those who will do the work. Directing is the process of communicating the plan, whether orally or in writing.

Figure 1-3. Planning Questions.

QUESTIONS	DOCUMENTATION
What is to be done?	Scope Definition document
Why should we do it?	Business Case or rationale
How should we do it?	Strategy and Work Breakdown Structure
In what sequence?	Network Diagram
Where should work be done?	Organizational Breakdown Structure
When should work be done?	Schedule Plan
Who should do the work?	Resource Utilization Plan
How much should it cost?	Cost Plan or Budget Plan
How do we judge progress?	Milestone Plan or Earned Value Plan

Organizing

Organizing brings together the nonhuman resources needed to achieve the project's objectives. To organize is to manage the procurement life cycle. It begins with the need to define requirements for material, equipment, space, and supplies. It also identifies sources of supply, ordering, reception, storage, distribution, security, and disposal activities.

Staffing

Staffing brings together the human resources. From a managerial perspective, human resources are first seen as the number and mix of individuals in terms of skills, competency levels, physical and logical location, and costs per unit of time.

Controlling

Controlling is the process of measuring progress toward an objective, evaluating what remains to be done, and taking the necessary corrective action to achieve the objectives. In project management terms, it involves determining variances from the approved plan, then taking action to correct those variances.

Coordinating

Coordinating is the act of synchronizing activities to ensure they are carried out in relation to their importance and with a minimum of conflict. When two or more entities compete for the same resource—time, space, money, people, etc.—there is a need for coordination. The primary mechanism of coordination is prioritization.

Processes in the Life of a Project

The Project Management Institute, an organization dedicated to advocating the project management profession, has produced a valuable document called *A Guide to the Project Management Body of Knowledge (PMBOK® Guide).* This document provides a broad view of what project management professionals should know and what they do in performing their work. This guide identifies and describes the body of knowledge that is generally accepted, provides common project management terminology and standards, and acts as a basic reference for anyone interested in the profession of project management.

The *PMBOK® Guide* defines the major processes in managing a project in five groups:

1. *Initiating*: defining and authorizing the project
2. *Planning*: defining and refining the project objectives; planning the course of action to obtain those objectives
3. *Executing*: integrating people and other resources to carry out the project plan
4. *Monitoring and Controlling*: measuring and monitoring variances from the project plan and taking corrective action when necessary

5. *Closing*: formally accepting the result of the project and bringing the project to an orderly end

Each of these groups has a number of interrelated processes that must be carried out for the success of a project.

Knowledge Areas

Project management has its own set of terms and acronyms to learn. Some project management terms can apply to any project, regardless of size or origin. Other terms are more specific to science and engineering or information technology.

The *PMBOK® Guide* identifies nine areas that describe project management's knowledge and practice:

1. *Integration Management*. This area includes the processes and activities required to ensure that the various elements of the project are properly coordinated. It includes developing the project charter and plan, directing and managing the project, monitoring and controlling project work, controlling change, and closing the project.
2. *Scope Management*. This area includes the processes and activities required to ensure that the project includes all the work required—and only the work required—to complete the project successfully. It includes scope planning, scope definition, creation of a work breakdown structure, scope verification, and scope control.
3. *Time Management*. This area includes the processes and activities needed to ensure timely completion of the project. It consists of activity definition, activity se-

quencing, activity resource estimating, activity duration estimating, schedule development, and schedule control.

4. *Cost Management.* This area includes processes and activities that ensure the project is completed within the approved budget. It includes cost estimating, cost budgeting, and cost control.
5. *Quality Management.* This area includes the processes and activities required to ensure that the project will satisfy the needs for which it was undertaken. It consists of quality planning, quality assurance, and quality control.
6. *Human Resources Management.* This area includes the processes and activities required to organize and manage the project team. It includes human resource planning and acquiring, developing, and managing the project team.
7. *Communications Management.* This area includes the processes and activities needed to ensure timely and appropriate generation, management, and communication of project information. It consists of communications planning, information distribution, performance reporting, and managing stakeholders.
8. *Risk Management.* This area consists of the processes and activities required to conduct risk management and planning with the purpose of maximizing the probability and consequences of positive events and minimizing the probability and consequences of negative events. It includes risk management planning, identification, qualitative risk analysis, quantitative risk analysis, risk response planning, and risk monitoring and control.

9. *Procurement Management*. This area includes the processes and activities needed to acquire the products and services needed to perform the project work. It consists of procurement planning, contracting, requesting seller responses, selecting sellers, contract administration, and contract closure.

OTHER DEFINITIONS

Your success as a project manager depends, in part, on being a role model for your team. Part of that obligation is to know and use project management vocabulary correctly, thoroughly, and consistently. Below are some of the basic terms you should know.

- *Project objectives* are the quantifiable criteria of cost, time, and scope that must be met for the project to be considered a success.
- *Project scope* defines the work that must be done to deliver a product or service with the specified features and functions.
- *Critical success factors* are qualitative criteria statements describing what will make the project successful.
- *Critical success measures* define the quantitative attributes, features, or functions that measure part or all of the project's critical success factors.
- *Float* is the time an activity can slip from its early start without delaying the project finish date. It is equal to the difference between the early start and late start (or the difference between the early finish and late finish). Also known as *slack, total float*, and *path float*.

- *Goal* describes (usually in clear, simple, nontechnical language) the product, service, or result that a project is expected to create.
- *Risk* is an uncertain event or condition that could have a positive or negative effect on a project's objectives.
- *Contingency (or reserve)* is a provision in the project plan to mitigate the impact of a variance in cost or schedule.
- *Stakeholders* are individuals and organizations who are affected by or have an interest in the project. They may also exert influence over the project and its results. Key stakeholders common to many projects include:
  - *Project managers.* The individuals responsible for managing the project.
  - *Customers.* The individuals or organizations that will use the result of the project (usually a product or service).
  - *Project team members.* The group performing the work of the project.
  - *Project sponsors.* Individuals or groups that provide the authorization or resources for the project.
- *Activity* is a unit of work performed during a project. An activity usually has a duration, a cost, and resource requirements. Also called *task*.
- *Work package* is a deliverable in the lowest level of the work breakdown structure. A work package may be divided into the specific activities to be performed.

CHAPTER

–2–

Leading and Directing Project Teams

Chapter 1 established the essential terms, concepts, and context for project management. It examined the managerial dimensions of work and the contexts in which project management may appear. In this chapter, we focus on a skill complementary to management. This central skill is *leadership.* When you are the project manager, you must lead. In other words, you must influence the behavior of others to accomplish the goal.

You need to know what it is you want your followers and team members to do, convey that understanding to them, contribute to their motivation, and remove the barriers to their success. To interact with others and to influence their behavior, you must first understand yourself.

Academic literature, reinforced by your own experience, confirms the importance of the interpersonal skill set in all collective endeavors. The purpose of this chapter is to improve your ability to lead. By the end of this chapter, you will be better able to lead your project team. Specifically, you will have enhanced your ability to:

- ❑ Describe the functions of leadership
- ❑ Lead others by communicating, motivating, and solving problems
- ❑ Give direction to others
- ❑ Manage work

Leadership Aspects of Project Management

There are two aspects of this chapter that need to be clarified before continuing: *concept* and *context.*

Conceptually, two ideas need to be explored. The first is that people who are given authority, accept responsibility, and are held accountable for the results they achieve and the resources they expend are in positions of command. People in positions of command will be more successful if they can manage and lead. The second idea centers on the relationship that exists between the activities of management and leadership. Management is the application of intellect to the functions of planning, directing, organizing, staffing, controlling, and coordinating. Leadership is the art of influencing others to accomplish the objectives desired by the leader. Leadership is not management or science. Leadership can be learned and is goal focused. Leadership sees only identifiable individuals—people with names and faces. One cannot lead a building, a budget, a software application, or an organization chart. Two people plus a common goal is a call for leadership.

In terms of *context,* we need to clarify the context in which leadership is explored in this book. Although the focus of this chapter is leadership, leadership is a component of all parts of this book. You will find references throughout the text to activities that involve your interaction with your subordinates.

To aid you in isolating the leadership component within the remainder of this text, remember that whenever you are dealing with identifiable individuals, you are within the leadership context.

Leadership Skills

Leadership skills are essential for project managers because project managers must influence the behavior of others. Project managers require leadership skills for the simple reason that they accomplish their work through people who have faces and names. It would be folly to ignore the contribution of the leadership skill set to the success of any project manager. In truth, leadership is the predominant contributor to the success of the ad hoc project manager. In small projects, good leadership can succeed even in a climate of otherwise unskilled management.

In project management's relatively brief history, there has been a keen shift in the relative importance of different skills for project manager success. We see that when selecting project managers, the leadership component is of significant value and that its relative importance is on the rise (see Figure 2-1).

Leadership Theories

Theories of leadership abound, but they all relate in one way or another to influence and motivation. The following is a partial list of leadership theories you may want to explore further:

- Great man theory
- Situational Leadership®
- Leadership contingency model
- Path-goal leadership theory
- Four-factor theory of leadership
- Substitutes for leadership
- Transactional leadership model
- Charismatic theory of leadership
- Transformational leadership theory
- Role theory
- Vertical linkage dyad
- Vertical exchange theory

Leadership theories can be categorized into three general sets: trait-based theories, situational theories, and relationship (or leader-follower exchange) theories (see Figure 2-2 on page 22).

Figure 2-1. Project Management Skills for Success.

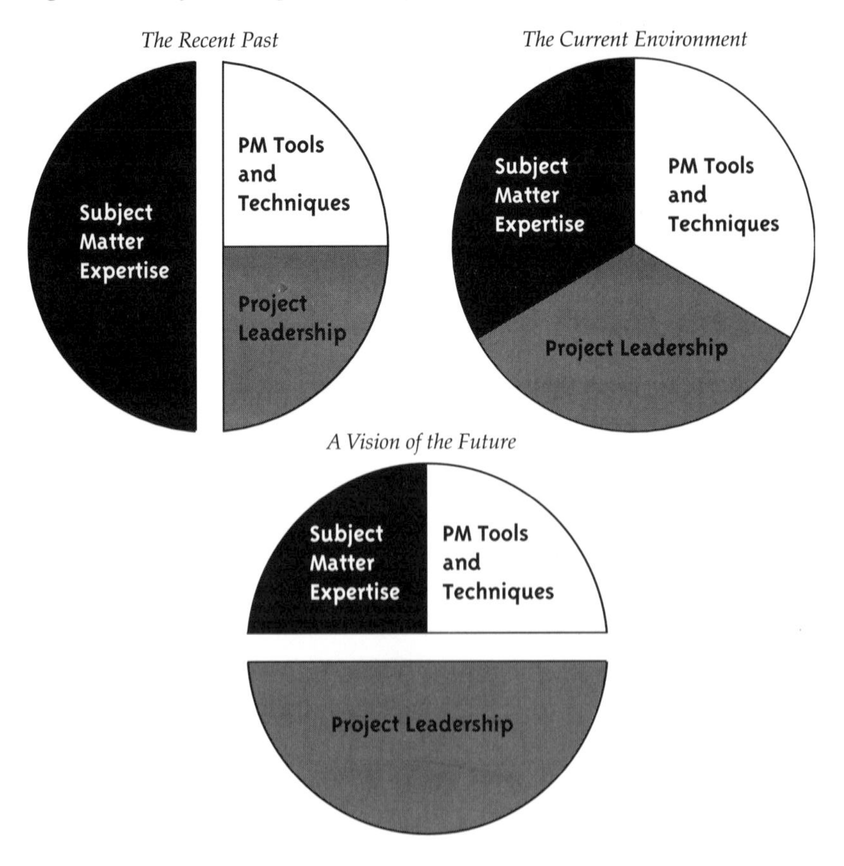

Trait

Trait theories of leadership focus on the personality and intellectual and physical traits that distinguish leaders from nonleaders. The majority of trait theorists agree that leaders have the following five traits in common:

1. Loyalty
2. Competence
3. Integrity

4. Conviction
5. Enthusiasm

Situation

In general, situational theories of leadership distinguish the leader from the nonleader through the situation; leaders emerge to fit the situation. Situational theories conflict with trait theories of leadership by identifying the importance of the group, but few deny absolutely the importance of the personal characteristics of the leader.

Situational theories give weight to the environment—that is, the organizational structure, the immediacy of the situation, and the capabilities of the followers—and demand that leaders alter their styles to accommodate the re-

Figure 2-2. Leadership Theories.

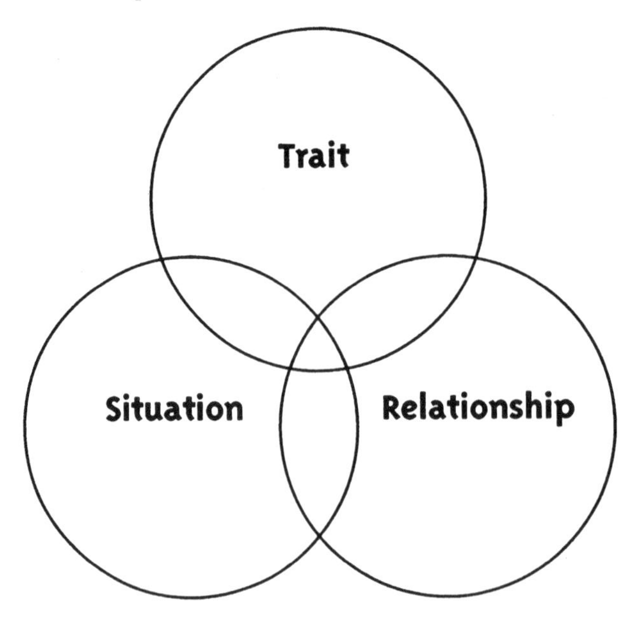

quirements of the follower and situation. Conversely, such theories also suggest that each situation will give rise to a different leader according to the demands of the moment.

Relationship

Relationship theories go one step further in stressing the importance of the group in determining the effectiveness of the leader. In leader-follower exchange theories, the leader-group relationship is directly related to productivity, esprit de corps, and other group dynamics. The exchange occurs in that the follower gives increased productivity in return for increased reward from the leader. Arguments abound within this set of theories about whether the relationship is between the leader and the group or between the leader and each member of the group individually. In any case, the more effective leader in this set of theories is the one who can best satisfy the needs of the followers. That leader will be rewarded with superior performance.

Unified Theory of Leadership

If a single unified theory of leadership existed, it would explain the role of individual characteristics and traits, the role of the situation (including the goal, organization, and culture), and the role of the leader-follower relationship (see Figure 2-3).

Within a unified theory, all activities would reduce to three fundamental functions of leadership:

1. *Communicate.* Convey information and evoke responses that indicate understanding.
2. *Motivate.* Stimulate another's performance in an activity.
3. *Solve Problems.* Overcome the obstacles to success.

Figure 2-3. Unified Theory of Leadership.

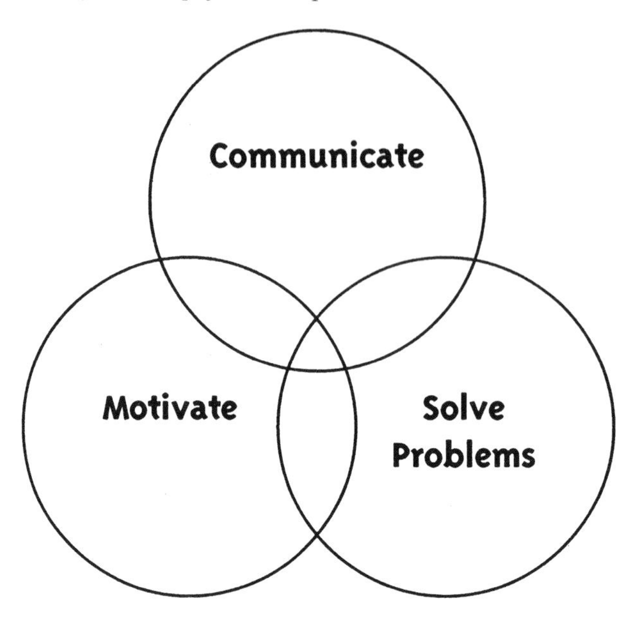

Leadership Functions

The leadership functions to communicate, motivate, and solve problems are interconnected. There are also two activities required of leaders that relate directly to the functions of leadership. These activities are to direct others and to manage them. The functions and activities of leadership are described in detail below.

Communicate

Communication involves eight fundamental factors:

1. Intent
2. Sender
3. Encoder

4. Message
5. Medium
6. Decoder
7. Receiver
8. Effect

In the communication model shown in Figure 2-4, each element is distinguished by characteristics, roles, and behaviors. The sender is someone who has composed a message to be shared. All receivers will share the message, but not all receivers may be members of the sender's target audience. Communication can be intercepted or misdirected. All that is needed to link receiver to sender is access to a common vehicle or means of communication. The message is the content.

The effect of the message depends upon three closely related elements:

Figure 2-4. Communication Model.

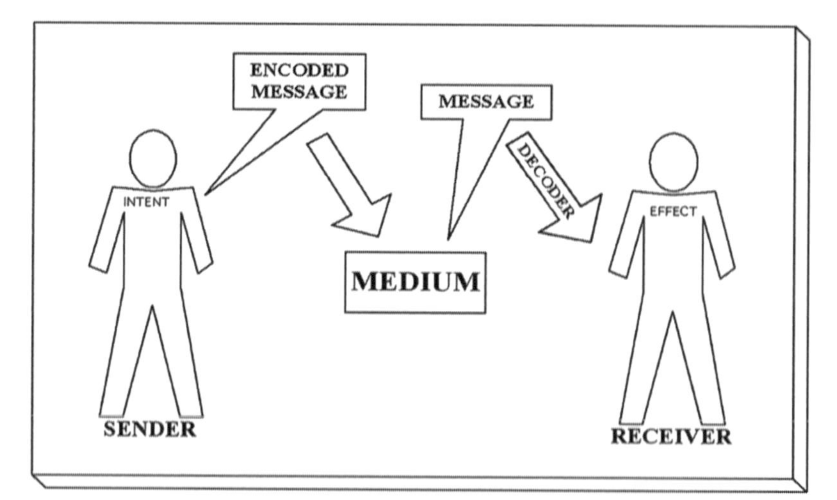

1. The sender's ability to incorporate within the message those stimuli that will evoke the desired effect
2. The medium's distortion of the message
3. The receiver's sensitivity

For instance, if the sender desires to communicate to the receiver the message "Come here," the sender has nearly infinite options—each of which will likely evoke a different effect. The sender encodes the message in a language either understood or not understood by the receiver, realizing that the not-understood language will not evoke the desired effect.

The sender selects a medium to which the receiver has access. The sender could prepare the message for transmission by sound using voice directly over short distances, by enhancement using a megaphone, by conversion and transmission by telephone, by telephone connected to a recording device, or by Morse code. The sender could prepare the message for transmission by sight using semaphore, sign language, a sign, a note, or flashing lights. The sender could use touch by sending the message using Braille or perhaps even send the message by smell using an attractant. However, none of these will achieve the desired result unless the receiver has access to and the ability to use the same medium.

The effect or result will vary according to the sender's ability to compose, to encode, and to use the chosen medium. The effect also depends on the receiver's ability to use the same medium, to decode, and to comprehend.

Synchronous communication involves transmitting and receiving information in real-time. For example:

- ❑ Face-to-face conversation
- ❑ Telephone conversation
- ❑ Instant messaging

Asynchronous communication involves some delay in the receiving of information by the receiver. For example:

- ❑ Voice mail
- ❑ E-mail
- ❑ Memorandum or letter

To communicate well is to write, speak, and listen well, along with the ability to read body language and other nonverbal cues. The use of tone, inflection, metaphors, and examples are also important in communicating effectively. One must be clear, concise, and complete to be understood. Leaders communicate person-to-person and with groups. Find ways to communicate that will appeal to the entire audience. That may mean drawing pictures, sending e-mail, talking over the telephone, or addressing an assembly. Using words and grammar incorrectly will lead to misunderstanding. The responsibility to overcome barriers to communication normally rests with the sender. However, in a leadership situation, the responsibility falls to the leader in all cases, whether one is sending or receiving.

Motivate

Motivation requires that you know yourself and know the people you are trying to motivate. Several tools exist that will provide insight into individual personality and preferences. Exploring these instruments may enhance your knowledge of yourself and others.

Your professional competence is a necessary precondition to your credibility. Your ability and willingness to set the example is a motivator. Avoiding situations because you do not know how to act or because you are fearful will not endear you as a leader. By the same token, you do not have to be able to do the jobs of your followers. You must be able to do your own job.

Your actions must also be beyond reproach. If you make an error, you must admit it readily, explain the results, and overcome the consequences. However, there are instances when a single error can damage your credibility to a degree that it cannot be regained. Reproachable behavior is contextual—it varies between organizations and cultures. What is acceptable in one instance may well be damnable in another. In this era of globalization, there is increasing opportunity for cultural confrontation. Whether you have individuals from other cultures under your control or you are working in a culture foreign to your own, the opportunity for unintentional errors with unimaginable consequence is significant. Prepare yourself for diversity through knowledge and understanding.

Your presence is needed as a manager. You must know what and why, who and how, and when and where. It makes you more able to respond to change, to learn from the past, to foresee potential risks, and to mitigate them. As a manager, be consistent and fair. Reward your subordinates publicly and correct them privately. Never pass a fault; never fail to praise. Your needs should be satisfied last as you strive to fulfill the needs of others. You need to give others the room to perform and to back them up when required.

Leaders work to motivate individuals in an organization. Here is your greatest challenge. All of your understanding, credibility, good intentions, and effort may fail to motivate anyone when the organizational context creates unresolvable demotivators. A corporate climate of poor pay, lack of recognition, long hours, faulty tools, impractical bureaucracy, misguided prioritization, intolerance, or unreasonable expectations can quickly defeat your best efforts.

Solve Problems

Leaders who say, "Don't bring me problems; bring me solutions" are abdicating their roles. It is the responsibility of the leader to solve the problems that cannot be solved by subordinates. It is also the responsibility of the leader to provide subordinates with the tools and techniques that will enable them to solve problems—and thus the number of problems that are elevated for resolution is minimized.

Problem solving is part mechanics and part creativity. Mechanically, the process is to:

- ❑ State the aim
- ❑ State the problem
- ❑ Analyze the problem
- ❑ Create viable options
- ❑ Apply evaluation criteria
- ❑ Choose the best course of action
- ❑ Secure necessary approvals
- ❑ Implement the solution

Creativity is essential to the production of viable options. In some problem-solving models, you will find that solving the problem ends when the viable options have been created. In such models, the remaining steps are categorized as selection or decision making. Here is an example:

> Many years ago, my wife asked me to remove a big, ugly rock from the backyard. In my mind, the aim was clear: Make the rock go away. The problem would continue as long as that rock was visible to my wife. I began to analyze the situation by examining the rock—its location, size and shape, relationship to the rest of the world (namely, my wife), and finally, the interrelationship of these factors. By answering a series of ''So what?'' questions, I came to understand the components of the problem.
>
> It was at this point that I set about creating as many viable solutions as I could:
>
> - ❑ Removal
> - ❑ Burial
> - ❑ Camouflage
> - ❑ TNT
> - ❑ Hammer and chisel
>
> To decide among the viable options, I removed from my wallet my *Standard Set of Criteria for Household Solutions.* On it were written these words: ''Of the available solutions, choose the one that most fully satisfies these criteria: Cheapest, Simplest, Fastest, Least Likely to Fail, and Least Disturbing to the Neighbors.'' This memory aid had served me well over the years and would not fail me this time. Having made my choice, I commenced

implementation in the usual manner, and the rest—as they say—is history.

When the solution to your problem involves bringing together a number of individuals, there is an opportunity for synergy. That is, the opportunity for the collective solution to be more viable, workable, practical, and successful than that derived from the analysis of any one of the same people working alone. Synergy occurs when the whole is greater than the sum of the parts. The probability of achieving synergy depends on the capabilities and characteristics of the individuals, their expertise, their willingness to work together, the size and structure of the group, the mechanisms of communication and collaboration, and the manner in which decisions are made. When conditions demand and synergy is attempted, and when conditions are right and synergy is achieved, the result is rewarding.

Direct Others

Leaders give direction to others. It is inherent in the relationship and is a communicating and motivating activity. There are four simple, common-sense steps to giving direction to others: *plan*, *prepare*, *deliver*, and *confirm*.

To *plan* is to answer who, what, when, where, why, and how. To *prepare* is to put into place the conditions for success: that is, arrange for the necessary resources, such as tools, equipment, facilities, funds, and people. To *deliver* is to express the desired action so it will be fully understood and work can begin without delay. To *confirm* is to ensure that there has been understanding. In the simplest, yet all-inclusive form, this could be the template:

> In order to achieve [why], I need [who] to [what] at [where] by [when]. I have arranged for [tools, equipment, facilities, funds, or people] to be made available to you. It is [imperative, likely, desirable] that the work be undertaken [how]. Is there anything I need to clarify? Do you have any questions? Get back to me by ________ should you have any questions.

This could now be delivered in person or by electronic or written means. You should choose personal delivery if your presence will add to the delivery of the message or if questions are likely to arise immediately. Choose electronic or written means if your presence is not required to reinforce the delivery, if the receiver will need time to digest the contents, or when the consequences demand complex instructions. In some cases, you may choose to deliver the direction personally while providing a hard copy. In all cases, the planning and preparation processes are important.

Manage Others

Management is also a motivating activity. There are three simple common-sense steps to managing people: *observe, react*, and *evaluate*. To *observe* is to watch the work or the results of the work while it is in progress. To *react* is to intervene when issues, problems, or new requirements arise and you need to make changes in your direction or in the work. To *evaluate* is to judge the results and feed this judgment back to the individuals who have done the work in order to improve future work. You must actively manage to be aware of the need to correct either the direction given or the work undertaken.

Conducting Meetings

Meetings expend time and effort—yours and that of others. Time and effort expended should return value. Meetings are a mechanism of leadership, but are dependent upon the functions of management. You must plan, organize, direct, staff, control, and coordinate in order to communicate, to motivate, and to solve problems. This is your orchestra and you are the conductor.

As a project manager, you will be required to conduct all types of meetings, including:

- ❑ Routine and regularly scheduled staff meetings
- ❑ Management briefings
- ❑ Interviews
- ❑ Critical design reviews; major milestone reviews
- ❑ Status reporting meetings
- ❑ Meetings with clients
- ❑ Meetings with independent oversight and regulatory bodies
- ❑ Meetings with vendors, suppliers, and other third parties
- ❑ Meetings that respond to local interest groups
- ❑ Quality control of intermediate and final deliverables
- ❑ Crisis meetings

This section reviews key elements that can help you conduct successful meetings of all types. Specifically, the concepts, tools, and techniques in this section will help you conduct meetings by determining participants, setting agendas, directing discussion, and summarizing results.

Stages of Meetings

Typically, meetings have three stages: planning, conducting, and postmeeting follow-up. The fundamentals of all meetings are the same, no matter the subject or participants.

Planning

It is important to plan for a meeting by doing the following:

- ❑ Establish an objective prior to the meeting.
- ❑ Write an agenda for the meeting, following the established objective. Describe the topics in sufficient detail and include estimated times for topics to be covered. For example, "Decide to accept or reject the marketing proposal number twenty-seven attached to this agenda."
- ❑ Determine the start and end time for the meeting.
- ❑ Determine the necessary participants and invite only those needed to achieve the objective.
- ❑ Assign a scribe to take minutes of the meeting, especially the decisions and assignments.
- ❑ Assign a moderator or facilitator, if needed, in addition to the person conducting the meeting.
- ❑ Distribute the agenda and supporting documents to participants prior to the meeting. Give them sufficient time to review the documents and come prepared for discussion and action.

Conducting

Your role in conducting a meeting includes the following:

- ❑ Start the meeting on time, according to schedule. Do not delay the start for latecomers.
- ❑ State the objective of the meeting and briefly review the agenda.
- ❑ Follow the agenda items. Encourage discussion of the topic at hand and discourage discussion of items not on the agenda. If a new issue is raised, offer to hold a separate meeting to address it.
- ❑ At the end of the meeting, summarize the points discussed, decisions made, and assignments given.

Postmeeting Follow-Up

After the meeting has concluded, be sure to do the following:

- ❑ Distribute minutes of the meeting and lists of assignments as soon after the meeting as possible.
- ❑ Periodically hold meeting reviews to evaluate the effectiveness of your meetings. For example, you could distribute a questionnaire to request feedback.

Meeting Checklist

The following questions may help you improve the effectiveness of your meetings.

Before:

- ❑ Is the meeting objective clear?
- ❑ Is this meeting necessary? Could the objective be reached in some other way?
- ❑ Who must be in attendance to achieve the objective?
- ❑ Where will the meeting be held? Is this convenient for the attendees?
- ❑ When will the meeting be held? Is this convenient for the attendees?
- ❑ Who will take the minutes?
- ❑ What will the seating plan be? Is this ideal for the objective of the meeting?
- ❑ Will there be refreshments and, if so, what should they be?
- ❑ If audiovisual equipment is needed, has it been scheduled, and are you sure it will be set up on time?
- ❑ Can the agenda and supporting documents be distributed early enough to give participants sufficient time to review the documents and come prepared for discussion and action?
- ❑ Have there been premeeting discussions with selected participants to address the potentially contentious issues?

During:

- ❑ Is the meeting starting on time?
- ❑ Are the topics beginning and ending on time?
- ❑ When topics surface that are not on the agenda, are they being recorded for future action?

- ❑ At the end of the meeting, do you summarize the points discussed, decisions made, and assignments given?

After:

- ❑ Are minutes of the meeting and lists of assignments distributed soon after the meeting?
- ❑ How often do you request feedback from the participants on the effectiveness of your meetings?
- ❑ How many items above were not done for this meeting? How can you improve for the next meeting?

Conducting Information Interviews

Interviews are common tools for collecting information in project work. At the project's outset, interviews clarify goals, objectives, and requirements. Early in the execution phase of the work, interviews may help document workflows, operations, problems, and opportunities. In the control stages of a project, interviews are used to determine status, variances from the plan, and opportunities for corrective action. In addition to their use as fact-finding tools, interviews can reveal other important elements in a project. Specifically, they may point to personality and political conflicts, they may illuminate hidden agendas, and they may uncover potential breakdowns or breakthroughs early enough to intervene in a helpful way.

This section of the book has been included to help you identify and define different types of interviews that may arise in a project context and to teach you the appropriate techniques to get the information you need from different stakeholders.

Interviews, like all meetings, have a specific purpose. Interviews are used to draw out as much information as possible on a specific topic. Interviews may be easier with a project team member who is readily available and with whom you already have a relationship and know the individual's personality and primary objectives. Interviews may be more difficult with a stakeholder you don't know who is not readily available. You may only have one or two opportunities to interview such a person. In this case, it will be important to prepare in advance, carefully target your questions, be flexible, and allow proper time to handle surprises that may come up during the interview.

Interview Checklist

Advanced preparation is key to successful interviewing. A preparation checklist is provided below.

- ❑ Make a complete list of potential interviewees.
- ❑ Know their job levels in the organization and their job functions.
- ❑ Decide whether to interview individually or in a group.
- ❑ Write questions tailored to the issue. Include both closed-ended and open-ended questions.
- ❑ Pretest your questions with similar parties within your own organization.
- ❑ Prepare your list of questions with sufficient space to record the answers.
- ❑ Prepare a separate file folder for each interview (person or group).

- ❑ Prepare the client for the interviews.
- ❑ Determine in advance the most appropriate location for the interview.

Technical Questions

When you have to ask technical questions, be sure you ask them of the individuals who have the technical understanding and experience to properly answer them. Ask these questions early in the interview because they are easier to answer, will put the interviewee at ease, and you will be sure to get them answered before running out of time.

General and Organizational Questions

Use general and organizational questions to draw out cultural, communication, and organizational issues. Senior managers should receive a higher proportion of these questions. When interviewing senior managers, keep organizational questions specific and strategic. End users and technical staff can handle questions worded more generally in this area. These people will gladly tell you what's going on at their earliest opportunity.

Ask the general questions later in the interview, when the interviewee is more open. For most end users and technical staff, the problem won't be getting them to open up; the problem may be in keeping them from running over their time.

Respect the time of the interviewee. Senior managers may only offer you fifteen minutes for an interview. Other project personnel may have more time available. Some may have a vested interest in "lobbying" you and may try to monopolize your time. You may want to prepare an exit strategy for each interview.

Becoming an Active Listener

Keep interviews as short as possible while still getting the information you need, and giving the interviewee time to bring up all the issues. Technical staff and end users may view you as a potential rescuer and tell you all the things they believe management has done to them. Be wary of endless venting from interviewees. Listen to what is said as well as to what remains hidden. Ask open-ended questions in a variety of ways so you can confirm or validate responses. Periodically pause and use a technique called *reflecting*. For example, ''Let me make sure I've understood your last point. You believe that departments X and Y have sharp conflicts regarding the location of the pilot plant. Is there anything we need to add to this so I've got a complete and balanced picture of this issue?''

During the Interview

Follow standard meeting etiquette during interviews. At the beginning, review the purpose of the interview from your point of view and ask the other person for his or her purpose. Also review the general procedure and time considerations. Ask easy, closed-ended questions first. Be flexible. Don't hesitate to rephrase a question to get the information you need. Different words mean different things to different people. If you're not sure about an answer, paraphrase what you think you heard and ask for feedback. When dealing with technical staff and end users, be ready for an onslaught of issues they may be harboring.

After the interview, thank the interviewee for her time and honesty. Ensure her that her opinions are important and will be taken under consideration. Provide her with a means to forward more information to you if she thinks of anything after the interview process.

Consolidating Information After the Interviews

It may be tempting to ignore the postinterview processing. A common belief is that after listening to all of the interviewees, you know exactly what's going on. Although this may be partially true, generating statistics and sample answers from the interviews will be highly revealing and also add credibility to the results. For technical questions, use a database or spreadsheet to consolidate answers. For open-ended questions, derive a consensus by reading responses and select one or two specific examples that demonstrate the consensus.

Interview Summary

Figure 2-5 summarizes interview techniques.

Figure 2-5. Interview Technique Summary.

Project Scope Interview Summary						
	General Considerations		Types and phraseology of questions			
Interviewee	Time in Interview	Phrasing Questions	Sample Organizational Question	Organizational Question Specificity	Technical Question Specificity	Sample Technical Question
Senior Staff	15-20 Min.	Strategic	What strategies do you employ to facilitate communication?			How is plant efficiency?
Middle Managers	20-45 Min.	Tactical	Do you feel you have good communication between management and staff?			What is your typical throughput on your assembly line?
End user	30-60 Min.	Process	How is communication around here?			How many widgets per hour can you get out of this machine?

Part II

PROJECT PLANNING

CHAPTER

–3–

Defining Project Scope and Requirements

The project manager is responsible for achieving outcomes and results. Therefore, the project manager must understand and convey the project's overall goal, objective, or vision. The project manager is the steward of the project scope. Even when the project manager inherits a project where the project triangle has been predefined and there are few degrees of freedom, the first obligation of the project manager is to validate the project scope.

The aim of this chapter is to help you understand how to define the scope of your project and secure broad agreement on the scope and objectives from key stakeholders. It will discuss the tools, techniques, and skills to develop or validate a secure, realistic, and achievable scope of work. At the highest level, the scope of work is defined in clear, simple, nontechnical language. Later in the process, the scope of work is developed and refined through the use of feasibility studies, requirement definitions, and extensive lists of end-item features, functions, and performance characteristics. It is important to document the scope of your project in terms of how it is today and what it will be when the project is completed. During the planning phase, you should also establish critical success factors and critical success measures. You will also learn the right tools and processes to define project scope. Chapters 1 and 2 gave you a basic vocabulary for project management terms and concepts. More terms will be added in Chapters 3 through 9.

ESTABLISH GOALS AND OBJECTIVES

Establishing or confirming your project's scope is the first critical step in running a successful project. This emphasis on early definition of a project's goal or purpose is not merely good theory and common sense. Evidence shows that project schedules and budgets overrun when the scope is unclear or when it is not aligned with enterprise goals, core values, structure, strategy, staff, and systems. Hooks and Farry (2001) examined several programs at the National Aeronautics and Space Administration (NASA). For each project, they calculated two items: the percentage of time the project team spent in designing a product before it was built and the percentage cost overrun for all projects. Without worrying much about the names of specific programs, please look at Figure 3-1. What conclusions can you draw? It is obvious in this sampling that the projects that spent more time in design had fewer overruns.

The process by which goals, objectives, and requirements are set may be simple or complex, trivial or traumatic. In all cases, it is best done by the project team, with the sustained participation of all interested and affected parties. Figure 3-2 suggests a high-level approach to scope definition.

Establish Time, Cost, and Performance Objectives

Scope definition should also establish time, cost, and performance objectives. The *PMBOK® Guide* offers two related definitions for scope. *Product scope* includes "the features and functions that characterize a product, service, or result." *Project scope* includes "the work that needs to be accomplished to deliver a product, service, or result with the specified features and functions" (*PMBOK® Guide,* third edition, 104).

Project scope management includes five processes:

1. *Scope planning* develops a project scope management plan.
2. *Scope definition* creates a project scope statement.
3. *A work breakdown structure* creates a hierarchical breakdown of activities and end products, which organizes and defines all the work to be completed in a project.
4. *Scope verification* achieves formal acceptance of the project scope.

5. *Scope control* creates a change control system to manage the project scope.

There are two countertendencies in defining project scope. One impulse is to constrain the project by insisting on near-total definition and documentation before any real progress is made. This may cause the project to be in a planning limbo from which it may not escape. The focus is

Figure 3-1. The Relationship Between Planning and Cost Overruns (Hooks and Farry 2001, 10, Fig. 1-4).

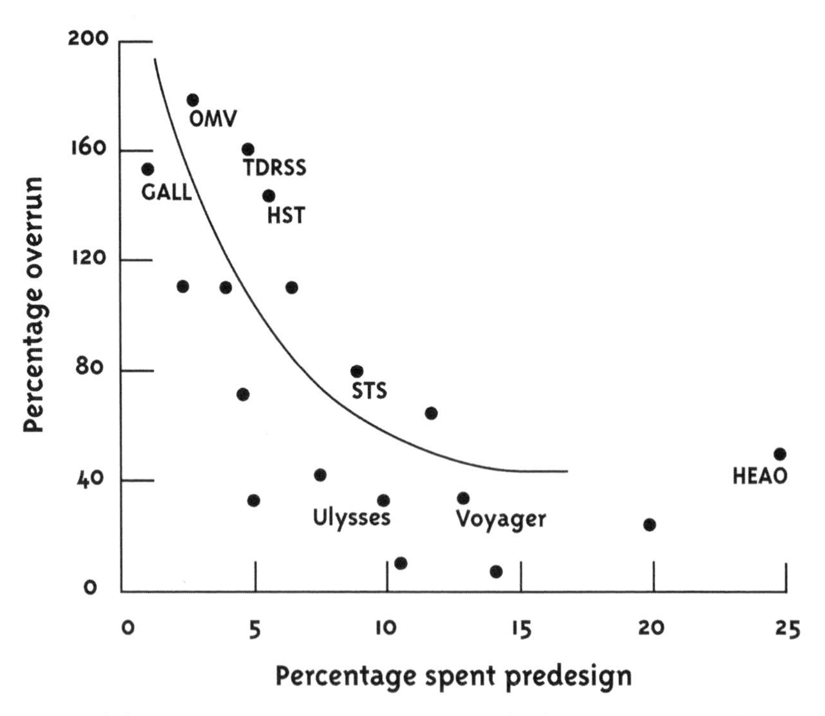

Figure 3-2. Scope Definition Process.

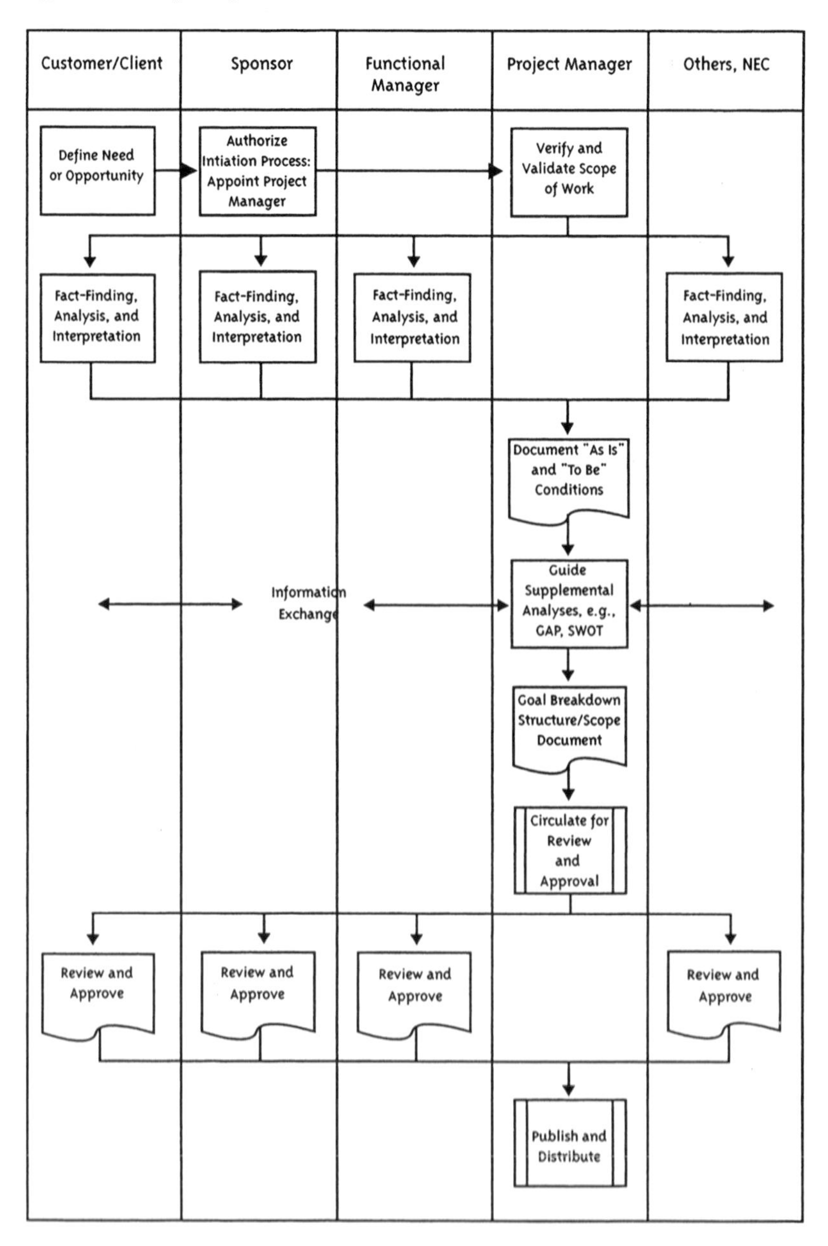

to continue planning, even though market forces may make the project increasingly irrelevant. At the other extreme, the tendency is to "hit the ground running," feeling there is no time to plan. This school of thought fails to understand the role of planning. The purpose of planning is not to produce a plan, it is to guide thoughtful implementation and execution in order to achieve the desired outcome.

In determining the project objectives, it is critical to recognize what drives the project. Some projects are driven by schedule. This means that a completion date is fixed and the other sides of the project triangle (cost and scope) can to some degree be negotiated. In other projects, the most important drivers are budget or scope. The following are reasons to understand what drives the project:

- Project drivers influence all dimensions of project planning.
- Project drivers help guide your selection of corrective actions.
- Project drivers assist you in controlling proposed changes to project scope, schedule, or cost.
- Project drivers help create appropriate management reserves and contingencies.

The notion of placing constraints on a project leads to the need for a practical tool that documents, early and often, a project's hierarchy of objectives and expectations.

Goal Breakdown Structure

The goal breakdown structure (GBS) is a logical and hierarchical structure that demonstrates, at increasing levels of detail, the results that a project should achieve. The specific names shown in this hierarchy are representative, not mandatory. Use terms that apply to your enterprise or organization. The following is one scheme you could use in a GBS:

- *Level zero* defines the project's *goal*—a clear, nontechnical description of the desired result or outcome of the work. Some organizations define the highest level of a project or program as the project's *requirement*, but other organizations use words like *mission* or *vision*. What is important is that everyone agrees on the outcomes sought.
- *Level one* defines project *objectives*—generally no more than five to ten essential attributes or characteristics of the project's goal statement. Taken together, these objectives document the project's *critical success factors* (CSFs), which are statements of qualitative criteria describing what will make the project successful. For example, the statement "Minimize time to completion" is a critical success factor.
- *Level two* defines the *requirements* or the *critical success measures* (CSMs) of the product, service, or process being designed and developed. CSMs are statements of quantitative criteria, each of which provides a measure of one or more of the project's CSFs. For example, the corresponding CSM to the CSF above would be the statement "Complete by January 6, 2015."
- *Level three* establishes the *specifications* for intermediate and end items of the project. Specifications can be thought of as detailed descriptions of how something

will work and its relationship(s) to its nearest neighbors.

The generic concept of GBS levels is shown graphically in Figure 3-3. Figure 3-4 shows the GBS levels in the familiar Noah's Ark project.

Let us now look at more-recent project examples to illustrate this idea. Figure 3-5 is a starting point for GBS development with three illustrative projects: one in marketing, one for information technology, and a third for an imaginary medical device.

Consider the following as you develop the goal breakdown structures:

Figure 3-3. The Goal Breakdown Structure (GBS).

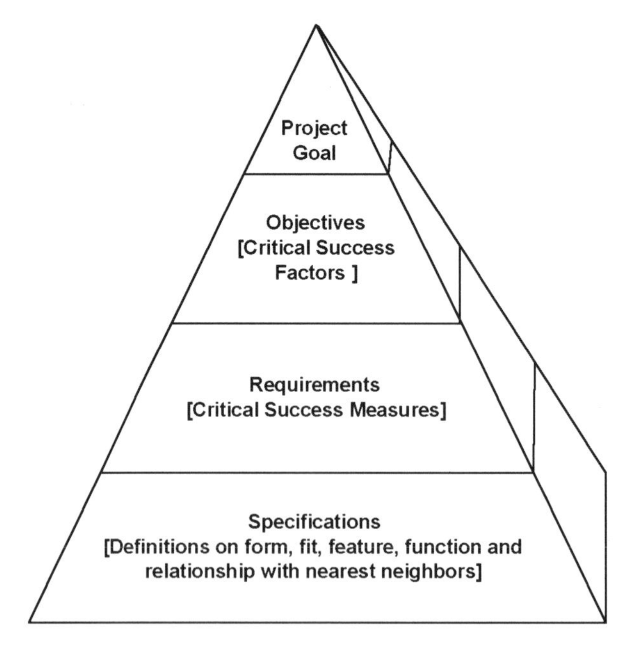

Figure 3-4. Goal Breakdown Structure Levels in the Noah's Ark Project.

GBS Level	Name	Example and Illustration
0	Goal	**Build an Ark**
1	Critical Success Factors	1. Maximize species survivability 2. Maximize durability 3. Complete on time
2	Critical Success Measures	1.1 Provide life-supporting quarters for 2x2 (or 7x7) based on type of species 1.2 Demonstrate ability to float upright for a minimum of 6 months 1.3 Complete by scheduled start of rain date
3	Specifications	1.1.1 Dimensions shall be 300 x 50 x 30 cubits 1.1.2 The ark shall be constructed of gopherwood 1.1.3 Interior and exterior sealants shall be pitch

Figure 3-5. Detailed Goal Breakdown Structure.

GBS Levels	General Business Project	Information Systems & Technology Project	Scientific, Engineering, & Technical Project
Illustrative Goal Statements	Double market share of left-handed doodads by the end of 2010	Install the newest release of the Operating System used in our configuration	Improve the sensitivity of a diagnostic test to detect PM pedo-oralgia (project manager's foot-in-mouth disease)
Ilustrative Objectives (Critical Success Factors)	1. Market size 2. Market share 3. Retention rate(s) 4. Satisfaction rates 5. Product quality	1. Timing 2. Continuity of operation 3. Compatibility 4. Security 5. Transparency	1. Accuracy 2. Speed 3. Cost 4. Reimbursable 5. Office-based
Example Requirements (Critical Success Measures)	1.1 From 25K/yr to 40K/yr 1.2 Capture 7.5% of new market 1.3 Achieve reorder rate of 75% 1.4 Achieve customer satisfaction rating of "best-in-breed" using J.D. Powers and/or Consumer Reports as benchmark(s) 1.5 Conform to applicable standards for left-handed doodads	1.1 Installed by 12-31-10 1.2 Downtime = 0 throughout install and cutover 1.3 New product must be compatible with current configuration's hardware, software, and net ware 1.4 No unauthorized CRUD, i.e., create, read, update, destroy information holdings 1.5 New release shall require no incremental training of technical, operational, or user staff	1.1 Less than 0.1% false positives or negatives 1.2 Less than 15 minutes from receiving sample until result is displayed and confirmed 1.3 Cost to manufacture shall not exceed \$15.50/test kit; target for gross margin is 45% 1.4 Employee health plans (and Medicare) will cover this test/service 1.5 Test can effectively, efficiently, and safely be performed in physicians' offices
Specification	TBD	TBD	TBD

- Senior management "owns" the goal statement. If it fails to endorse or support a fundamental statement of project purpose, your issues as project manager will be overwhelmingly political rather than technical, organizational rather than operational, and personal (and personnel) rather than scientific.
- Functional managers, users, and clients "own" critical success factors and their essential metrics. Deriving and documenting these items is likely to take more time and effort than you imagined.
- Subject matter experts (SMEs) "own" the specifications in the execution and implementation stages of the project. Expect robust debate and dramatic conflict when the worlds of SMEs collide!

Project Scope Document

A project scope document defines your project, including specifications, exclusions, constraints, risks, and assumptions.

Specifications

Specifications, by definition, are unique for each project. Nevertheless, they must also conform to applicable laws, standards, codes, and conventions, which may derive from sources such as the following:

- *Government agencies* may be international, national, state, or local agencies involved in regulating specific industries, the environment, health, safety, or transportation. Some agencies regulate standards, licensing, or zoning.

- *Industry-specific professional or trade associations* may develop codes, conventions, or standard practices. These associations and practices include the International Organization for Standardization (ISO), the American National Standards Institute (ANSI), Underwriters Laboratories Inc. (UL listing), Generally Accepted Accounting Principles (GAAP), Generally Accepted Auditing Standards (GAAS), the Software Engineering Institute (SEI), and the Project Management Institute (PMI).
- *Your own organization* may have standards for data names and uses, numbering schemes for engineering drawings, or a visual identity program to guide the use of the company logo.
- *Your customers, clients, or end users* may impose their standards on your work; for example, "The contractor shall prepare and submit all engineering drawings as [name of product] files."

The standards that apply to your project should be developed early in the development of specifications. They should be articulated by subject matter experts, embedded in the scope document, and used later on to judge the quality of intermediate and final deliverables.

Exclusions

An adequate scope document defines not only what the project includes, it also establishes project exclusions. This delineation, although seldom perfect, forces stakeholders to confer openly and candidly in the early stages of a project. The project manager guides this dialogue. Its product is a scope definition with clear boundaries, diminished uncertainty, and minimal likelihood that the project manager will hear (at the end of the assignment), "I know it's what I said, but it's not what I want."

Scope exclusions define items that may be closely related to the project's goal but are not to be included in this phase, stage, or release. Exclusions may extend to piece parts, specific features and functions, materials, and performance measures. The important issue is that these exclusions be identified early, debated openly, and resolved with finality.

Constraints

Constraints are items that limit the project manager's degree of freedom when planning, scheduling, and controlling project work. Often, these constraints are administrative, financial, or procedural in nature. The following are examples of constraints:

- There is a hiring freeze for specific positions.
- The project has a capital-equipment ceiling of $500,000.
- The team must use an executive's brother-in-law as the architect.
- A vice president must approve all travel.

Risks

Risks are discrete events that may affect the project for better or worse. These events may be categorized in various ways, but their central theme is that one cannot predict with certainty the source, timing, impact, or significance of specific risks. Therefore, at the start of a project, it makes sense to undertake a high-level risk assessment by identifying the sources and types of uncertainty.

The initial assessment of risks to the project involves three steps:

1. Identify the risks likely to impede project progress and success.
2. Rank each risk in terms of the likelihood of occurrence and the impact on the project if the risk occurs.
3. Develop an initial list of responses for the risk that have unacceptable outcomes.

Figure 3-6 illustrates a simple and convenient way to present the results of this initial, high-level risk analysis.

Assumptions

Assumptions are made to fill in gaps of credible knowledge, to simplify complex realities, and to get others to

Figure 3-6. Risk Probability and Impact.

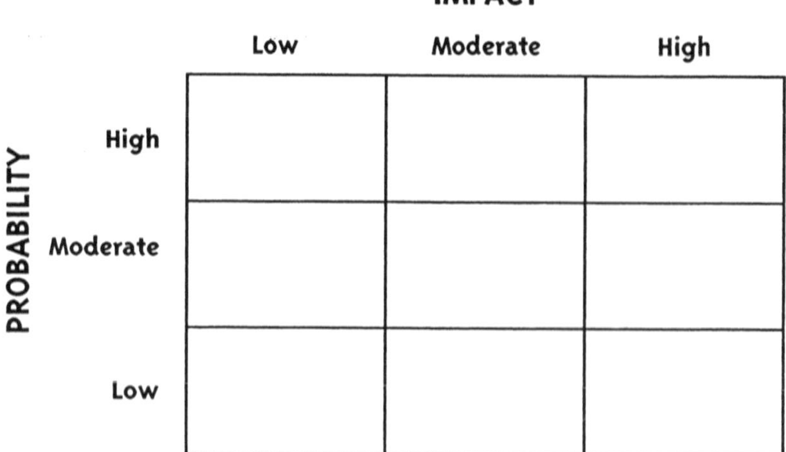

react. One way to categorize assumptions is to group them under one of four headings:

1. *Technical and scientific assumptions* routinely deal with hardware, software, or related configuration issues. We can postulate change or stability. In designing an experiment, we might assume that ten tests will be required or that a certain number of patients must be enrolled to achieve some level of confidence in results.
2. *Organizational and administrative assumptions* typically deal with roles and responsibilities, issues of outsourcing versus internal development, or make-or-buy decisions. By extension, they may address applicable standards for documentation or the tenure of project staff at the end of the project.
3. *Resource and asset availability assumptions* address issues regarding whether adequate numbers of people, materials, supplies, space, and equipment are available to meet project requirements. This set of assumptions requires the project manager to revisit some of the organizational assumptions noted above.
4. *Macrolevel assumptions* are those that are so profound or pervasive that project managers cannot negotiate them in any meaningful way. We could include here issues of currency fluctuations, exchange rates, public policy, population migrations, and related demographic trends.

Time, Cost, and Performance Trade-Offs

The scope document should address the trade-offs among time, cost, and performance. Conventional wisdom says:

"You may want it good, fast, and cheap. Pick two!" Underlying this aphorism is an intuitive grasp of simple points:

- ❑ If the technical requirements of a project are fixed, then compressing the project schedule will probably increase project costs.
- ❑ The more the schedule is compressed, the greater the rate of increase in cost per unit of time.
- ❑ If you add requirements to the scope, then either time or cost (or both!) will increase.
- ❑ If the project budget is fixed (as by legislative appropriation or a fixed-price contract), then negotiation arises on the other two sides of the project triangle (time and scope).

Visualizing these relationships is straightforward and shown in Figure 3-7. The graph shows the range of cost-versus-time solutions for a given project scope. For any project, there are three critical data points:

1. The earliest finish date of the last activity
2. The latest allowable finish of the last activity
3. The least cost to accomplish all the work required

By extension, we can find a point that describes the *late finish* and *last dollar*. This point is the sponsor's expectation that she or he will receive the final product or service on or before a given date and at a cost not to exceed some predefined amount. The area between any point on the time/cost trade-off line and the outer limits of the project is a management reserve or contingency for the project manager. Now the drawing looks like that shown in Figure 3-8.

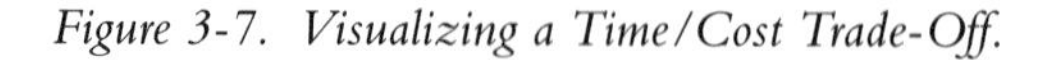

Figure 3-7. Visualizing a Time/Cost Trade-Off.

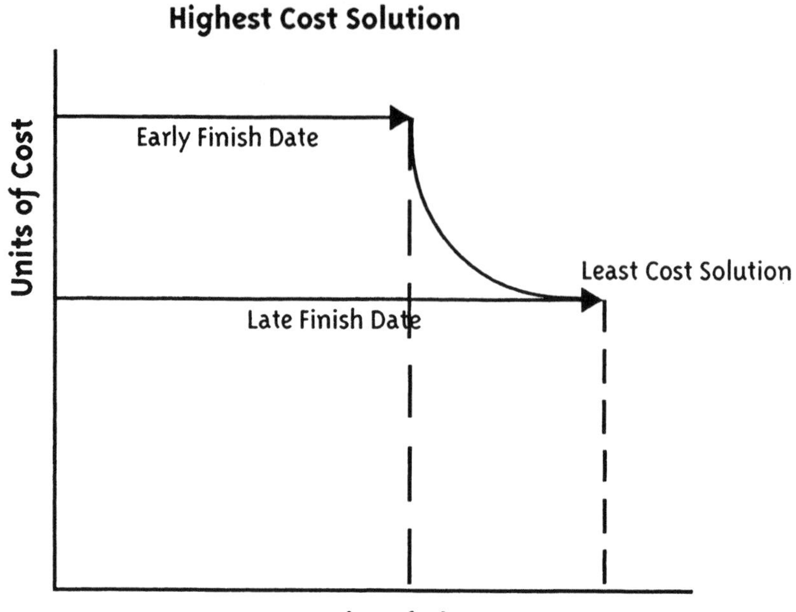

The project manager can now present the options to senior management and other stakeholders. Problems will only arise when the project budget is less than the cheapest solution or the needed delivery date is sooner than the fastest solution.

Tools to Use in Preparing a Scope Document

There are several methods you can use to establish or confirm a project's scope. The tools listed in this section are not exhaustive and should be tailored for each project and

Figure 3-8. Project Limits and Contingency.

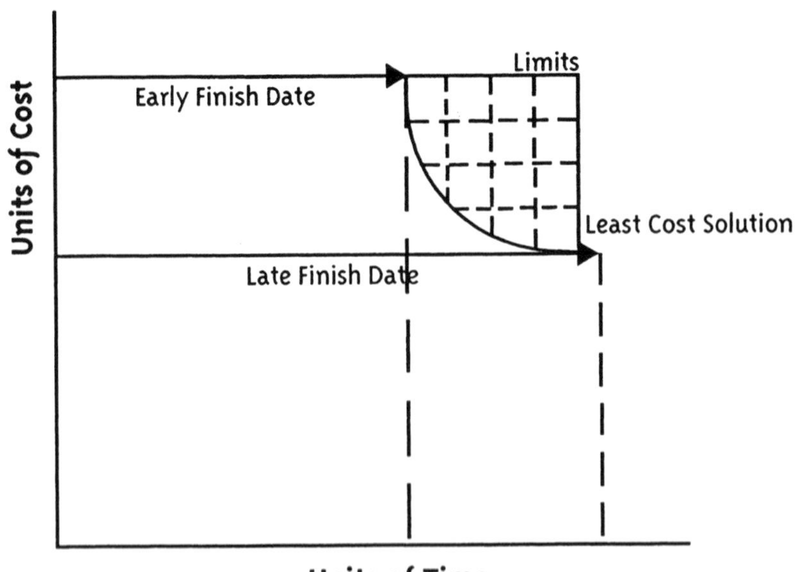

its unique context. These methods are neither mutually exclusive nor inflexible. Use multiple techniques and adjust them as needed to meet the specific parameters of both the project and the stakeholders' cultures.

Interviews

Interviews are the most traditional means of establishing project scope. The typical steps for conducting interviews include the following:

- ❑ Identify and select appropriate stakeholders to interview.

- ❑ Create an appropriate instrument for the interview.
- ❑ Schedule interviews. Confirm beforehand and acknowledge afterward.
- ❑ Conduct interviews.
- ❑ Compile and analyze results.
- ❑ Create project scope.
- ❑ File working papers.

Interviews may be done both informally or formally and are tailored to each type of stakeholder. Interviewing techniques are discussed in Chapter 2. Your skills can be improved with practice.

Gap Analysis

Gap analysis is routinely used for business-process reengineering, quality improvement, ISO certification, cost reduction, and efficiency-improvement projects. This approach has the following key elements:

- ❑ Determine the desired status or process (the to-be condition).
- ❑ Determine the current status or process (the as-is condition).
- ❑ Determine the difference between the two.
- ❑ Develop a strategy to bridge or fill the gap.

The following is an example of a gap analysis on the project of hosting a dinner party:

- ❑ *Step one: Determine the desired status.* The desired outcome is that the necessary food, condiments, and supplies are available in sufficient quantity, quality, and time for the event. Special attention should be paid to dietary needs based on religion, tradition, or health needs of your guests.

- *Step two: Determine the current status.* The current situation is found by taking inventory of pantries, refrigerators, and freezers.
- *Step three: Determine the difference between the two.* In essence, subtract the as-is list from the to-be list.
- *Step four: Develop a strategy to fill the gap.* The difference is your shopping list.

SWOT Analysis

A SWOT analysis is a review of the internal and external environment to determine the Strengths, Weaknesses, Opportunities, and Threats. This is a classic tool used in strategic planning and capital budgeting. At the project level, it may provide a rationale or justification for the project, or it may uncover important information that is helpful in matching the organization's resources and capabilities to the competitive environment in which it operates. Strengths and weaknesses are environmental factors internal to the organization; opportunities and threats address external or market issues.

Walk-Throughs

The project team can conduct a walk-through or site inspection of the client's processes in order to understand the business process and to document data flow, materials, supplies, and correspondence. This is helpful when the project involves replacing a process, usually through automation, and for process improvement. Walk-throughs are particularly helpful when they can be combined with operations data, such as that dealing with complaints, response times, and rejects.

Creativity Tools

There are many creativity tools that can assist in developing a project scope. Brainstorming is a technique used for problems that resist traditional forms of analysis. The goals of a brainstorming session are to stimulate the generation of ideas and, thereafter, check them for potential use. The key characteristic of a brainstorming session is that there are no wrong answers. An affinity diagram can then be used to refine the results of the brainstorm by organizing the ideas into related groups.

Mind mapping is a tool for processing information in both serial and associative forms. One begins with a central idea and then asks teammates to identify and list whatever comes to mind, periodically regrouping the ideas under headings that seem natural and appropriate.

Other Tools

There are many other tools and methodologies that can help you confirm a project scope. These include flowcharts, process reviews, data reviews (such as financial, operational, and managerial audits), models, simulations, competitive intelligence, focus groups, and literature searches.

Alignment with Business Goals and Strategies

A project charter or business case has several characteristics. The single most important characteristic deals with alignment of the project objectives with the business goals and strategies of the organization. Ask yourself the extent to which a particular project is aligned along these parameters:

- Business goals and objectives
- Business strategies and timetables
- Corporate culture, core values, and beliefs
- Organizational structure
- Operating policies, practices, and procedures
- Business systems
- Professional and ethical standards

SMART Objectives

One important aspect of establishing client and stakeholder expectations takes into account the difference between well-defined objectives and poorly defined ones. Although several models exist, one of them asks if the project objectives meet the SMART test, that is, are they Specific, Measurable, Agreed upon, Realistic, and Time/Cost limited? The SMART model is designed to minimize misinterpretation or vague assumptions in the project scope document. Figure 3-9 lists the characteristics of SMART objectives and provides a brief description of their implementation.

Fuzzy Objectives

Frequently, the project manager will be faced with the situation that a client cannot or does not fully understand what he or she wants. A similar issue exists when a client and internal stakeholders are in conflict regarding the project

Figure 3-9. SMART Objectives.

Characteristic	What it Does	Why it Works
Specific.	Makes objectives so clear and well-defined that anyone with a basic knowledge of the project area can understand them. Objectives must precisely define what the project will and will not do.	Forces you to search for precision. Removes ambiguity and forces hidden agenda items into view. It clarifies erroneous assumptions.
Measurable.	Forces objectives to be defined in measurable terms. If they cannot be measured, they are too ambiguous and need to be defined more clearly. It establishes project metrics for success early.	Defines the quality measure against which the objective can be evaluated—it either meets the standard or it does not. Allows you to measure and report on the progress.
Agreed upon.	Ensures that all stakeholders agree on the project objectives before the project begins. There must be agreement that the end result will solve the problem or respond to the opportunity defined.	Establishes expectations and reduces politics.
Realistic.	Ensures that sufficient resources, knowledge, and skills are available to complete the objective.	Helps prevent cost and schedule overruns. Helps ensure project scope will be achieved.
Time/Cost limited.	Ensures that sufficient time/cost is available to achieve the objective. Defines how much time and budget is available and if there is any flexibility.	Establishes client and stakeholder expectations.

objectives. These situations create what are known as *fuzzy objectives*. A fuzzy objective is one that does not conform to the characteristics of a well-written requirement. The objective is not specific, measurable, agreed upon, realistic, or time/cost limited.

Frequently, clients and project managers create fuzzy objectives because of misunderstandings. Clients may not understand the technology or project teams may not understand the clients' needs. The following represent several helpful techniques:

- Define terms or use different terms to reach understanding and agreement.
- Concentrate on outcomes or desired results, not on process variables.

- ❑ Build working prototypes.
- ❑ Use acronyms sparingly.
- ❑ Avoid needless technical jargon.
- ❑ Reflect and revisit what you have heard.
- ❑ Use physical demonstrations or experiments.
- ❑ Document your agreements (early and often).
- ❑ Use idea-generating techniques like brainstorming or mind mapping.

Example Scope Document

We conclude this chapter with an example that consolidates the key themes and serves as a working model of a high-level scope document (and the thinking process that underlies its development). The example used here is simple and specific. It is not intended to show all possible scenarios, but it does provide a concrete example of how to develop a scope document. It captures the way a project manager thinks.

The case example begins when you receive this e-mail from your supervisor, the business-unit manager of the bridge-building company where you are an experienced project manager:

> I have another bridge project for you. Our biggest client, Glenfracas Distilleries, wants to move its product overland into a new market at the rate of 100,000 liters per week using its own ten-ton trucks. The River Why stands in the way. The company is already prepared to spend mid-seven figures, and our signed contract is for

a cost-plus-percentage fee. The client's major competitor plans to have product in the same market within three months. Take this ball and run with it. We can discuss your understanding of the project scope when I call you from Cancun tomorrow.

Although you may rather be in Cancun to discuss this project with the boss in person, it is time to ask some questions:

- ❑ *What is the client's goal?* Move product by road. So what? The River Why stands in the way.
- ❑ *What is the boss's goal?* Make money. Keep our biggest client happy. So what? At least he has signed a contract, but mid-seven might not be enough money unless we keep the costs down.
- ❑ *How does the client describe the finished product?* He doesn't . . . at least not yet. So what? Maybe I can make some assumptions: If a ten-ton truck carries ten tons, and one ton of product is approximately nine hundred liters, that means that the bridge only has to be available for eleven loaded trucks each week. So what? Maybe this bridge only has to be one lane wide, and maybe it only has to support one loaded truck at a time. So what? If I can assume that a loaded ten-ton truck is three meters wide, the roadway on the bridge only has to be a little bit wider than that. If I can assume that a loaded ten-ton truck weighs seventeen tons, the bridge only has to support that weight. Anything else? I'm going to assume that they have no specific location for this bridge. So what? Site acquisition will be a major—and risky—part of this project.

- ❑ *How does the boss describe the finished product?* He doesn't . . . at least not yet. So what? Looks like the bridge design is going to be a part of the project.
- ❑ *What is the current state of the client?* The boss hasn't mentioned anything new, so I can assume that Glenfracas is still doing well and still satisfied with our previous work for it. So what? If all goes well, there should not be any surprises from the client. It has always turned the approvals around quickly and has always taken our word for the engineering. So what? That will really help on the risk analysis.
- ❑ *What is the current state of our company?* We have a good track record and none of our union contracts are up for renewal. Our plate was full until earlier this year, but we are at about 80 percent capacity right now. So what? I should have no problem finding the project team and project resources that I need.
- ❑ *What is my current state?* In another two weeks, my role in the Glenwidget Tay River bridge project will be over, I just finished my annual vacation last month, and my evening classes for my postgraduate work do not start for another four months. Except for seeing our oldest off to the university next month, this project comes at a pretty good time.
- ❑ *Is quality an issue?* We have to meet government code, but if this is a private bridge there could be some leeway. Other than that, it will have to go all the way across the river and support the expected traffic. So what? There seems to be some opportunity for scope creep, but little room for surprises. And, in the end, this is not a constraint.

- *Is time an issue?* The boss hasn't set any deadlines, but the client's competitor seems to be moving into the same territory in the next few months. So what? I won't tie my project's success to someone else's actions, but it may be necessary to constrain this project to three months. That's another assumption to be checked.
- *Is cost an issue?* The boss hasn't set any cost limits, but knowing the parsimonious culture of this part of the world, I fully expect to have to minimize the frills. So what? That should help keep this project simple and quick.

So, in preparation for the discussion with the boss tomorrow, what have we got?

- The *project goal* is to build a "Bridge on the River Why."
- My *assumptions* that I will have to validate with the boss and the client are:
  - Time is of the essence.
  - A loaded ten-ton truck is three meters wide.
  - A loaded ten-ton truck weighs seventeen tons.
- The project's *critical success factors* are:
  - Complete the bridge on time.
  - Make it support a loaded ten-ton truck.
- The project's *critical success measures* are:
  - Complete the bridge within ninety calendar days.
  - Make it support seventeen tons.
- The obvious *project risks* are:
  - Insufficient time

- ❑ Regulatory denial
- ❑ Regulatory delay
- ❑ Environmental issues
- ❑ Geotechnical issues
- ❑ Site acquisition issues
- ❑ Vendor performance failures
- ❑ Resource availability

That ought to be enough until he calls tomorrow. I feel that I have a pretty good handle on what is in scope and what is not.

CHAPTER

–4–

Developing the Project Work Plan: The Work Breakdown Structure

This chapter introduces the central tool for effective project planning, scheduling, and controlling—the *work breakdown structure (WBS)*. If defining the project's goal is the heart of project management, then the WBS is the skeleton, musculature, connective tissue, and central nervous system. The WBS provides both structure (for stability) and articulation (for movement) to the project plan.

Creating the WBS is simple, but not always easy. The underlying concept is clear. A WBS describes, in outline form, the work needed to meet project objectives. The outline is logical and hierarchical, but not necessarily sequential. At its highest level, the WBS conveys an approach, strategy, methodology, template, or best practice routinely used in your type of project. At its lowest level of detail are unique work packages that must be performed.

The WBS is ordinarily displayed in a top-down manner. In actual development, a WBS may have some pieces developed top-down or bottom-up. In either case, as the WBS becomes increasingly detailed, work packages appear. These work packages will then be used to sequence the work into network diagrams, schedule work, assign resources and costs, and establish the definitions of appropriate quality for each deliverable that emerges from the project work.

Later on, in the execution and control processes, the WBS becomes a tool for reporting, communicating, motivating, and establishing accountability. Fortunately, there are generic forms of the WBS and, with experience, they will become well understood by the project team.

When complete, the WBS helps you execute, control, and close the project. If the WBS is incomplete, then the project manager has little hope of success. Specifically, if there is work that must be done but it is not in the WBS, the project will likely be late, over budget, exceed its resource usage, and be of diminished quality. The anticipated benefits will not be delivered, and the end result will be an upset sponsor or client.

The purpose of this chapter is to improve the skills you need to create a WBS. By the end of this chapter, you will be better able to create a WBS that is appropriate for your project, regardless of type or context. Specifically, you will be able to define and document the project work, develop project templates, define appropriate levels of work for groups, and determine the skills needed to achieve the work.

The Work Breakdown Structure Is an Outline

Project goals, objectives, and requirements are routinely documented in charters, business cases, and scope documents. Fundamentally, they answer the questions of ''What is to be accomplished?'' and ''Why are we pursuing this now?'' These questions ask for a description of the result to be achieved, its business or technical rationale, and the project's alignment with strategic business issues. Left out, so far, is the question of how best to meet our requirements or objectives. The answer to this last question puts us in the middle of the project planning process.

The central part of a detailed planning process is developing a WBS, which is a description of the work to be done—and only the work to be done—that meets the project's objectives. This description is traditionally done as an outline. The highest level of description embraces and includes all subordinate levels. The outline itself is logical and hierarchical, but not necessarily sequential. Here is a simple example of a WBS for a term paper:

1. Title
    1.1. Section
        1.1.1. Paragraph
            1.1.1.1. Sentence

Writing the report does not have to be done in section sequence. Nonetheless, each section has the same logical and hierarchical structure. The WBS is a template or guideline. It works independently of whatever report is being produced.

Let's look at another example. Suppose we have an out-of-the-ground engineering and construction project. One part of the project deals with land use. This portion of the project generates the following WBS by the project team:

1. Make land usable
   1.1 Conduct site surveys
   1.2 Obtain permits
   1.3 Clear site
   1.4 Excavate site
   1.5 Regrade and groom site

What happens between the end of "Excavate site" and the start of "Regrade and groom site?" A substantial portion of the work associated with construction, equipment installation, testing, and commissioning is done.

Work breakdown structures may be displayed either as lists or as graphical decomposition diagrams (which typically resemble organization charts), such as the one shown in Figure 4-1. Each level in the WBS is oriented toward groups of deliverables. Each level is complete only when all of its subordinate work items are done.

As a practical matter, the new project manager tends either to overstate or understate the degree of detail in early efforts to craft a WBS. When asked the question "How many levels of detail should be included in the WBS for my project?" the answer would be that it depends on several factors. Three issues determine the level of WBS breakdown:

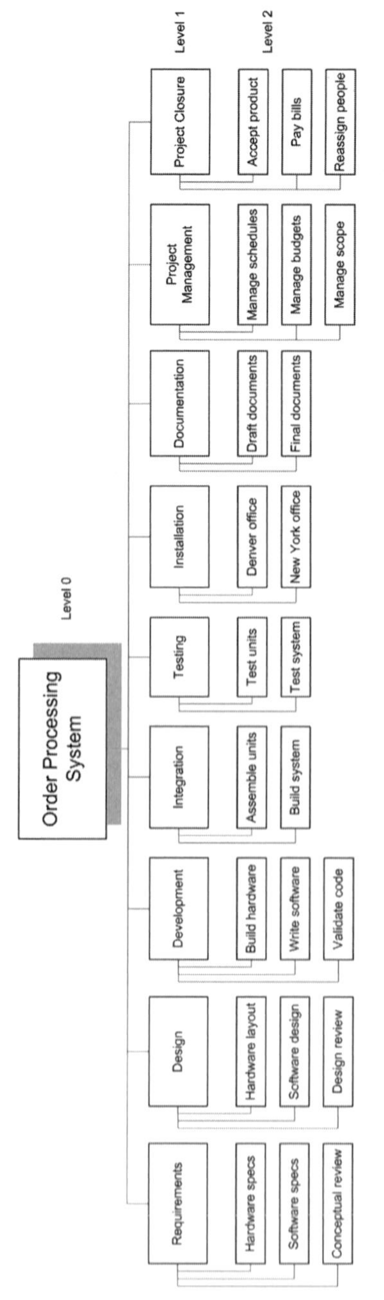

Figure 4-1. Work Breakdown Structure of an Order Processing System.

1. The level(s) of WBS detail should be dictated by the complexity and risk of the work.
2. The level at which you plan establishes the level at which, thereafter, you can control.
3. One person's project may be another's work package.

Phrased differently, the extent of WBS decomposition—that is, the number of indentation levels in the outline—depends on how you are going to use the WBS. The WBS is central to effective planning because it validates virtually every component in the project plan. The WBS is central to project control because it gives you the basis—and the detail—needed to measure and manage work.

The Work Breakdown Structure Is a Validation Tool

At its higher levels—usually levels one and two—the WBS describes and validates your project's approach or methodology. At these levels, the WBS is often broken into phases or stages. These are often viewed as pieces of work delineated by milestones, deliverables, or management decisions that authorize future work. In other words, the WBS summarizes all subdivided elements in your work plan.

The WBS is an example of a *functional decomposition* diagram. It is milestone (or deliverable or product) driven until its lowest level of *work packages* is reached. Thus, a top-down development approach yields progressively better-defined work products. A bottom-up approach is used to develop estimates. In other words, planning is done from a global level down to work packages. Estimating is done using work packages as units of analysis that are then aggregated to form project totals.

At lower levels, where subactivities and work packages emerge, the WBS serves several purposes:

- The *work package* (or lowest level of decomposition) is used to later define the logical sequence in which the activities could be performed in a *network diagram.* (Note: This is explained in detail in Chapter 5.)
- Planning-team members then use each work package as a basis for estimating. Each discrete piece of work will have estimates for duration, assets, resources, and costs. Team members should ask the following questions:
  - How long will it take to do the work?
  - How many asset and resource units will be required?
  - How much will it cost?
- Work packages can be used to capture technical and performance objectives. Each work package must produce some kind of deliverable or product. In fact, a work package is not complete unless a following activity accepts its product. Therefore, when you create a customized WBS for your project, you automatically create an index of deliverables—a master list of documentation items that flow from each piece of work. Each deliverable, in turn, has quality standards associated with it.
- The WBS can also be used to assign accountability and develop a responsibility assignment matrix for each work package and work product. This is a spreadsheet where work packages are in rows and organizational

units are the columns. The resulting cells can then be used to describe the relationship between work and performing organizational units. Figure 4-2 shows a simplified example. (Note: A more complete treatment of this topic appears in Chapter 7. There, we build an integrated project plan and one of its components is the project's organization plan.)

- The WBS can be seen as a foundation piece for project risk analysis. As the planning team develops the de-

Figure 4-2. Responsibility Assignment Matrix.

	Engineering Department	**Purchasing Department**	**Receiving Department**	**Accounts Payable**
1. Define Requirement	Primary; notifies Purchasing of potential need			
2. Prepare RFP (technical)	Primary	Reviews Engineering documentation		
3. Prepare RFP Bid Package	Reviews Purchasing documentation	Primary; focuses on T&Cs, non-collusive bidding		
4. Evaluate Bids (technical)	Conducts technical evaluation			
5. Evaluate Bids (cost and contract)		Conducts business and contractual evaluation		
6. Select Vendor (after negotiation)	Supports evaluation process	Issues PO to successful vendor; notifies Engineering and A/P		Creates A/P "dummy" record
7. Monitor Progress	Evaluates Work in Process	Processes Invoices		
8. Accept Final Product	Evaluates Quality of Product	Processes Invoices	Receives end item; notifies Engineering	
9. Authorize Payment	Validates Deliverable	Authorizes Final Payment		Issues Final Payment

tailed WBS, members can isolate those packages where uncertainty abounds. This will, in turn, affect estimating the work because team members must factor in the probability of occurrence and the likely impact of each occurrence.

- Not only is the WBS the foundation for detailed planning, it is also the centerpiece of controlling work in process, management reporting, change control (or configuration management), and closure. Simply put, the structure you use to plan the work in the WBS becomes the basis for tracking work performed, variance analyses, and corrective action.

Work Breakdown Structures Are Flexible

WBSs are flexible and adaptive tools. There is no single scheme that can be applied to all projects. In fact, even within a specific industry or for a repetitive application, the WBS may be customized to meet the particular needs of a project. The WBS may be tailored to account for geography, culture, language, social convention, or the names of particular components. A WBS may be shown in graphical format or in a numbered list.

In an ideal world, WBSs would preexist as templates or checklists and little modification would be required. Unfortunately, most of our projects begin with a high-level approach or strategy and then must be customized to meet unique project requirements. Therefore, it is helpful to look at WBS examples from various industries or businesses so that you can adapt them to your particular requirements or organization. We have developed several examples, each at a fairly high level, to indicate both the commonality of approach and the distinctiveness of specific project types.

The example in Figure 4-3 comes from projects that deal with plant expansions, line extensions, out-of-the-ground construction, or design-bid-build projects. In this example, the highest level of the WBS drawing represents project phases. This six-phase project may be adequate for senior management, but it lacks any real appreciation of specific work that needs to be accomplished.

Figure 4-4 shows the expansion of phase two to illustrate how that phase could be shown to four levels of detail. Please note that this example may be incomplete.

Where, for example, would we insert nuclear engineering or instrumentation and control subsystems in this example? Your project team would use this template to validate the project's technical objectives. It would expand the WBS to ensure that all technical objectives and requirements were properly addressed in this early version of the WBS.

In some technical projects, the WBS may develop in terms of piece parts or components. Each component then has work packages for design, building a prototype, testing, revising and refining, building a production model, and so on.

When projects are to be done at multiple locations, the first level of decomposition could be geographic. A country

Figure 4-3. Sample WBS for an Engineering Project (Strategic Level Only).

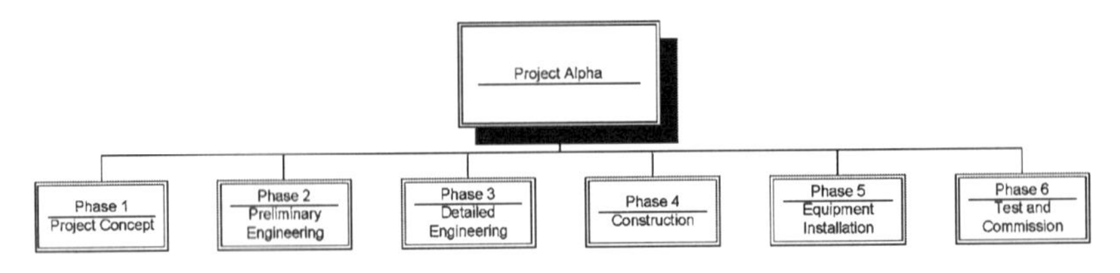

Figure 4-4. Sample WBS for an Engineering Project (to Four Levels of Detail).

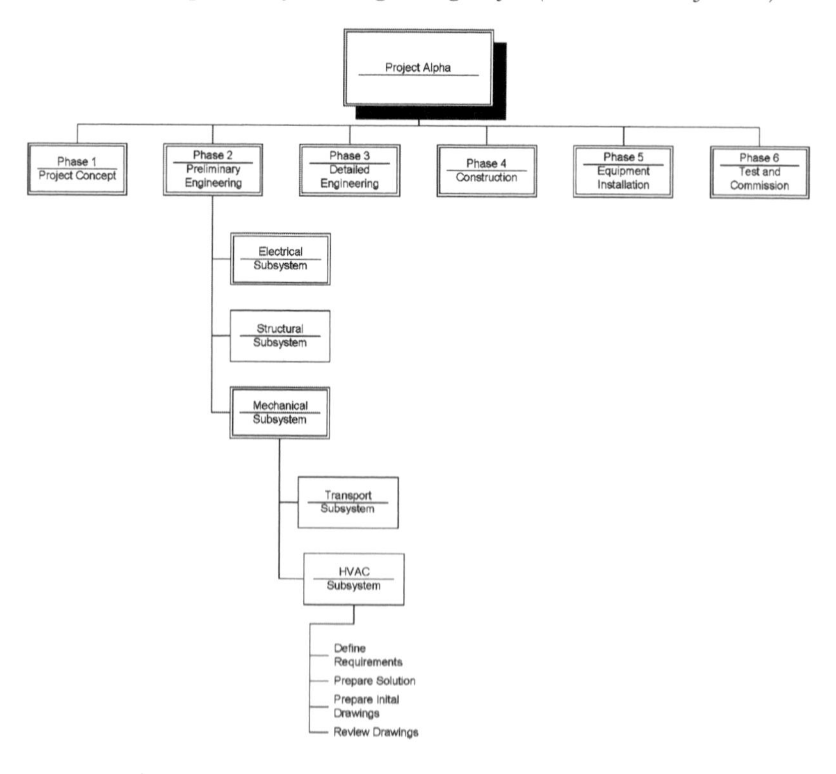

manager or site manager then becomes responsible for all the work packages performed under his or her direction.

Figure 4-5 illustrates a project that will develop and deploy an assembling machine. It assumes that proof of concept and proof of principal have been demonstrated. This figure shows a WBS in a list format.

The two preceding WBS examples presume a well-developed and familiar methodology. If, however, your project involves significant unknowns or operates at or near issues of basic science, research, or development, then your WBS model may resemble Figure 4-6.

If we expand the first part of this example, then the

Figure 4-5. Sample WBS for Product Design.

WBS No.	Description of the Work	Key Deliverable
1.	Phase 1—Product Design	Design document
1.1	Produce initial sketches and drawings	
1.2	Review and revise documentation	
1.3	Produce detailed line drawings	
2.	Phase 2—Build Prototype	Working prototype
2.1	Verify design documentation	
2.2	Assemble necessary materials	
2.3	Build working prototype	
2.4	Test prototype; create punchlist; repair defects	
3.	Phase 3—Build Production Model	Production model
3.1	Create bill of materials	
3.2	Purchase necessary items	
3.3	Build to print	
3.4	Conduct progressive testing	
3.4.1	Systems integration testing	
3.4.2	Systems acceptance testing	
4.	Phase 4—Deploy the Production Model	Installed system
4.1	Prepare facility	
4.2	Train operators	
4.2.1	Cold commissioning	
4.2.2	Hot commissioning	
4.3	Perform post-installation validation test(s)	

Figure 4-6. Design Experiment.

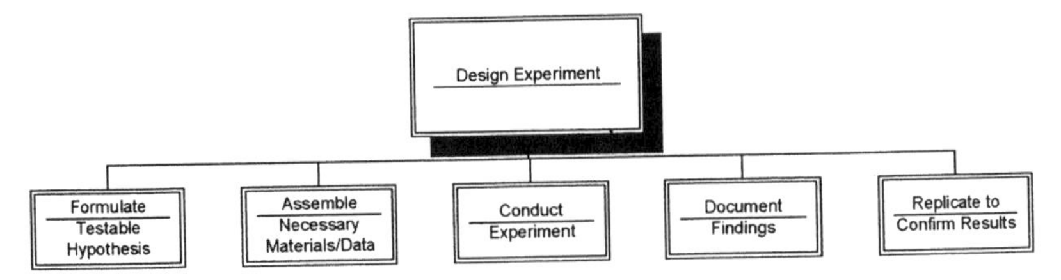

WBS might look like Figure 4-7 (in list format) or Figure 4-8 (as a graphical decomposition diagram).

Techniques to Create Work Breakdown Structures

Developing a customized WBS is both a radical and conservative exercise. It is conservative because it relies, whenever possible, on practical and proven ideas, tools, and techniques. It is radical because it forces the project team to examine the roots of its approach or methodology for this sort of project.

The following are some tools that might help your team create a WBS that addresses unique requirements of a project. These tools help project teams address scope ambigu-

Figure 4-7. WBS in List Format.

1. Formulate Testable Hypothesis and Research Design
    - 1.1. Conduct Literature Search
    - 1.2. Identify Design Variables
        - 1.2.1. Experimental Group
        - 1.2.2. Control Group
    - 1.3. Construct Research Protocol
    - 1.4. Secure Necessary Approvals
        - 1.4.1. Institutional Approvals
        - 1.4.2. Patients
        - 1.4.3. Participating Clinicians
        - 1.4.4. Oversight and Regulatory Bodies

Figure 4-8. WBS in Graphical Format.

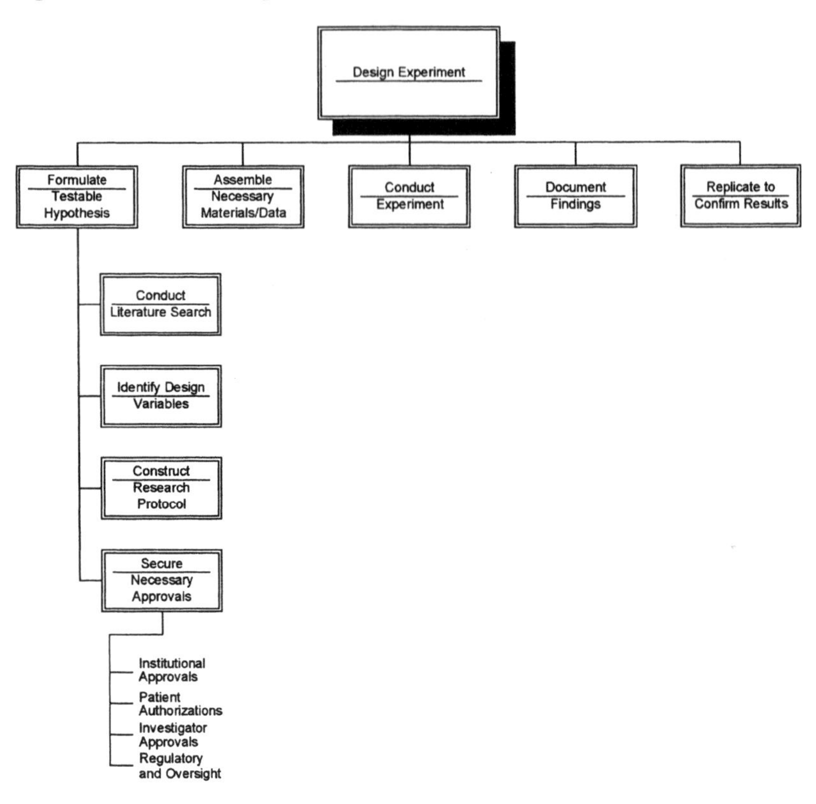

ities, overlaps and duplication, unrealistic expectations of one or more stakeholders, conflicting objectives, and differential priorities associated with requirements.

- Preexisting templates or checklists. These may include industry-specific or government-furnished checklists, best practices, guidelines, specifications, or standards.
- Internet downloads (often by industry or topic).
- Brainstorming or another idea-generating tool for use when a problem resists traditional analysis.

- Mind mapping and affinity diagrams, which are powerful tools reflecting the mind's ability to do (and use) associative, rather than purely serial, reasoning.
- Index cards to document and organize ideas, goals, roles, and responsibilities.

CHAPTER

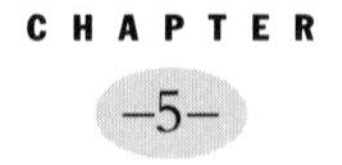

Defining Activity Dependencies and Creating Network Diagrams

In Chapter 4, you learned to create a work breakdown structure. This chapter will show you how to take the work packages from the WBS and build a logic network diagram that faithfully captures the relationships among the work packages discovered in the WBS. Remember that activities or work packages are small pieces of work that have clear organizational accountability and consume time, resources, and money. Work can be organized into milestone events, which represent major phases of the project. Milestones use no time, resources, or money.

To identify which work activities may be completed at the same time and which must be completed in sequence, you need to determine the relationships or dependencies among the activities. For example:

- *Physical or Engineering Dependencies.* For example, you cannot install a roof until the walls exist, hardware must be available to install software, and reagents must be available to conduct a specific experiment.
- *Resource Constraints.* Each piece of equipment, each person, each facility, and every dollar is subject to availability as to time, place, quantity, and quality.
- *Administrative or Operational Dependencies.* Sometimes work products must be approved before subsequent work begins. Frequently, such dependencies bring related requirements for exceptions, exemptions, appeals, permits, procedures, regulations, and statutes.
- *Dependencies of Convention.* Sometimes the order of work is merely traditional, doctrinal, or simply a matter of preference.

This chapter provides ways to portray dependencies. By the end of this chapter, you will learn to describe logical dependencies, create a logical network diagram, calculate forward and backward pass, calculate free and total float, and determine the critical path.

Network Diagrams Show Activity Sequence

A network diagram is a graphical display of the sequence in which activities will be performed. The basis of a network diagram is the project's work breakdown structure. Clearly, not all activities can be performed at the same time. The technique used to determine the logical sequence of work identifies and documents the dependency relationships between activities or work packages.

Ideally, network diagrams are constructed twice in the planning process. The first time a network diagram is built assumes the availability of all essential people, tools, equipment, supplies, and money. The resulting diagram illustrates the most natural and efficient sequence of work that accomplishes the project's objectives.

After this sequence appears, the project planning team then estimates the time needed for each activity in the network as well as the resources needed. This creates a *demand function* or a requirement for each resource by activity and time period. The demand function is then contrasted with supply or capacity for each resource. All too often, what results is a situation in which demand exceeds supply or requirements exceed capacity. The planning process then has several options. The most frequent solution—a form of resource leveling—adjusts the schedule so that it accommodates resource availability. A second option is to change the dependency relationships in the network diagram. This may lead to activity overlaps, activity splitting, or other less-than-optimal scheduling solutions.

One final point is that the act of examining network logic and dependency relationships can validate the project's WBS. Conversely, when your planning team begins to define predecessors for particular activities, you may discover that activities or work packages need to be added to the WBS.

Types of Network Diagrams

Although network diagrams can be drawn in many ways, one of three predominant types will likely serve you well.

Activity-on-Arrow

In the activity-on-arrow diagramming method, events in the project are shown as nodes (usually circles or squares), and the activities sit on the arrows. Figure 5-1 uses an activity-on-arrow diagram to illustrate part of a project that produces a report for management. In the diagram, node B is referred to as a *burst* or *source node* because it has multiple successors (activities 2, 3, and 4). Node F illustrates a *sink node* because it has multiple predecessors (activities 5, 6, and 7).

Precedence Diagramming

A second method of displaying dependency relationships is the precedence diagramming method. In this approach,

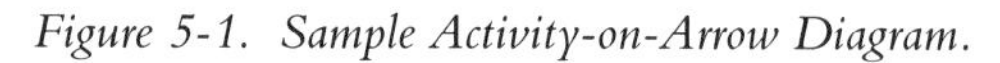
Figure 5-1. Sample Activity-on-Arrow Diagram.

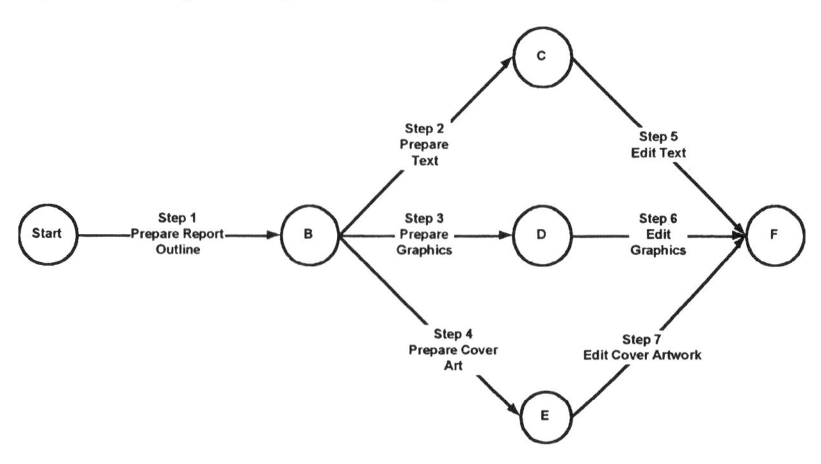

the nodes represent the activities and the arrows imply the milestones or deliverables from each activity. Figure 5-2 transforms the previous illustration from an activity-on-arrow diagram to a precedence diagram.

Conditional Diagramming

A third method of displaying dependency relationships uses a more sophisticated technique called conditional diagramming. This approach permits nonsequential activities such as loops or iterations as well as "if-then" branching. Loops and iterations typically occur in experimental design projects where you cannot easily predict the number of times a test will need to be performed or how many compilations will be required before error-free code is generated. Conditional branching arises after a test is done (often during quality-assurance or quality-control work) and the next steps are dictated by the results of the test. As a general rule, neither activity-on-arrow diagramming nor precedence diagramming permits loops or conditional branches.

Activity Dependencies

Activities may be dependent on one another in various ways. Some dependencies are mandatory (or hard logic) in that they are inherent in the nature of the work being done. For example, a construction superstructure requires a foundation, hardware must be available before software is loaded, and prototypes must be built before they can be tested. Other dependencies are discretionary (preferred, or soft logic) and are adopted by a project team because they reflect best practices within a particular subject matter area,

Figure 5-2. Sample Precedence Diagram.

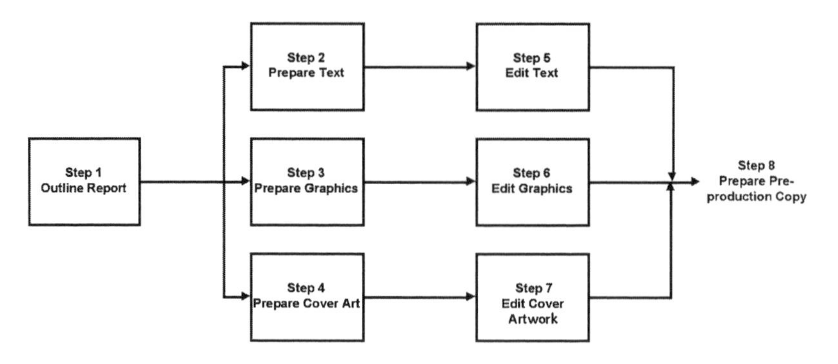

or because unique conditions suggest a specific approach. These dependencies should be used sparingly because they could limit future degrees of scheduling freedom. There may also be external dependencies that come from outside the project. For example, the testing activity in a software project may be dependent on delivery from an external source, or environmental hearings may need to be held before site preparation can begin on a construction project.

All activities in the network diagram must be linked using one of the following four relationships:

1. *Finish-to-Start (F/S).* Activity A must finish before activity B can begin.
2. *Start-to-Start (S/S).* Activity A must begin before activity B can begin.
3. *Finish-to-Finish (F/F).* Activity A must finish before activity B can finish.
4. *Start-to-Finish (S/F).* Activity A must begin before activity B can finish.

Of these four relationships, the first three are the most common. All four are illustrated in Figure 5-3.

Figure 5-3. Sample Network Diagram.

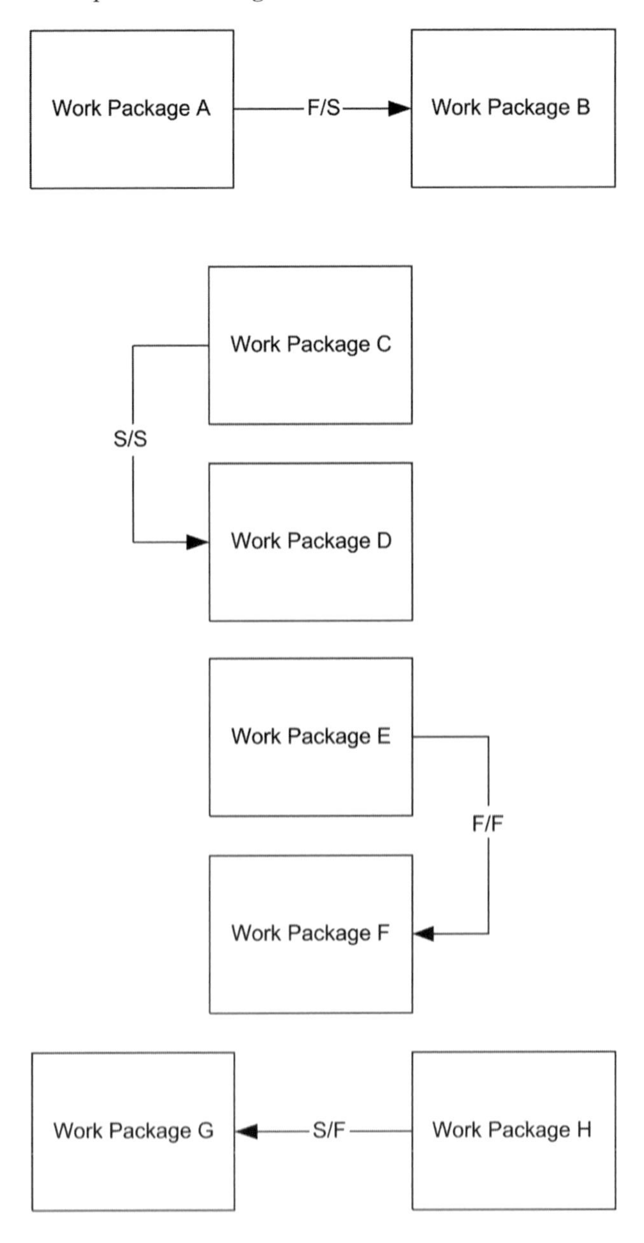

Project conditions may require that activities be further defined using indirect constraints such as the following:

- ❑ Must start on . . . (Activity must start on a given date)
- ❑ Must start before . . . (Activity must start before a given date)
- ❑ Must start after . . . (Activity must start after a given date)
- ❑ Must finish on . . . (Activity must finish on a given date)
- ❑ Must finish before . . . (Activity must finish before a given date)
- ❑ Must finish after . . . (Activity must finish after a given date)

Overlap or Separation of Activities

Many projects are schedule driven. That is, they must reach completion on or before a given date. One way to achieve schedule compression is to overlap activities that, ideally, should wait for a finish-to-start relationship. The following are examples of schedule compression by overlapping activities:

- ❑ Program coding begins before program specifications are completed.
- ❑ Prototypes are started before all subsystem engineering is done.
- ❑ Manuscript editing begins before the report is completed in draft form.

To build network diagrams for these situations, we must incorporate the following two concepts:

1. A *lead* relationship allows an acceleration of the successor activity. For example, in a finish-to-start dependency with a ten-day lead, the successor activity can start ten days before the predecessor is finished.
2. Conversely, a *lag* relationship defers the start of a successor activity. For example, in a finish-to-start relationship with a ten-day lag, a successor activity cannot start until ten days after the predecessor is complete. Lag can be helpful to schedule a waiting time needed (for example, the curing time needed after pouring concrete).

Figure 5-4 shows a lead relationship (with generic units of time) and Figure 5-5 illustrates a lag relationship.

Figure 5-4. Lead Relationship.

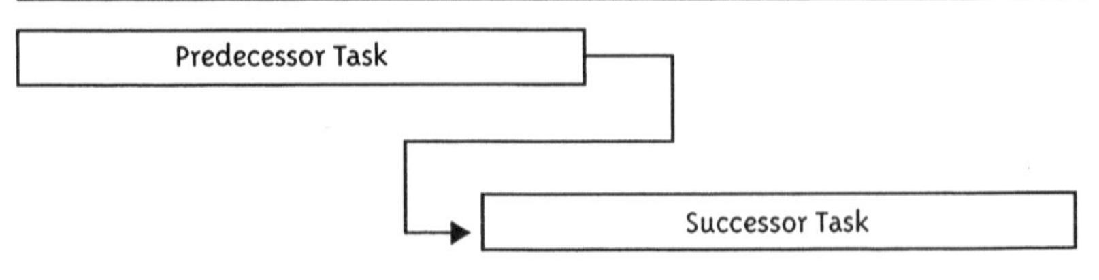

Figure 5-5. Lag Relationship.

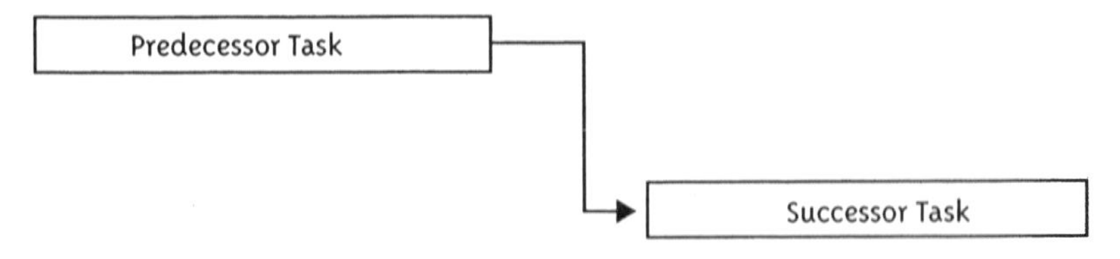

Sample Network Diagram

Let us put all this good information to use in a practical example. Imagine a project with nine work packages. The relevant information for each work package is found in Figure 5-6.

Using this information, you could draw the network diagram shown in Figure 5-7.

Critical Path

The *critical path* is the path through the network that takes the longest total time. It therefore determines the earliest possible time the project can be completed. Activities on the critical path are not inherently more important than other activities in the project, but they are more critical to the overall project schedule, because any delay in them will delay the completion of the entire project unless other adjustments are made.

The critical path allows the project manager to under-

Figure 5-6. Data Entry Requirements for a Network Diagram.

WBS No.	Description	Duration	Predecessors
1	Project Summary		
1.1	Work Package A	5 days	—
1.2	Work Package B	2 days	1.1 F/S
1.3	Work Package C	3 days	1.1 F/S
1.4	Work Package D	1 day	1.2 F/S
1.5	Work Package E	3 days	1.1 F/S
1.6	Work Package F	8 days	1.3 F/S
1.7	Work Package G	3 days	1.4 F/S
1.8	Work Package H	6 days	1.6 F/S
1.9	Work Package I	5 days	1.5 F/S; 1.7 F/S; 1.8 F/S

Figure 5-7. Network Diagram Solution.

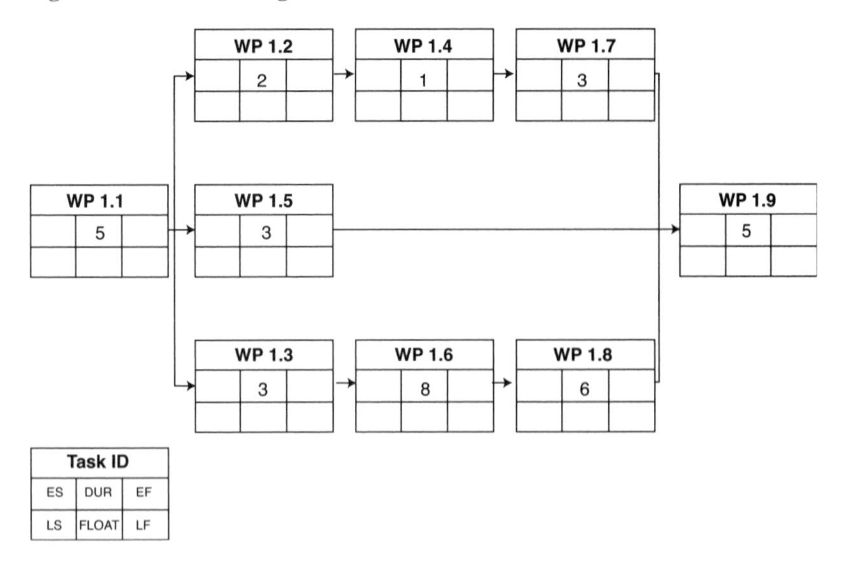

stand which activities have schedule flexibility and which do not.

Calculating Critical Path Dates

The critical path method calculates the following dates for each activity:

- *Early Start*: the earliest date the activity can begin
- *Late Start*: the latest date the activity can begin and still allow the project to be completed on time
- *Early Finish*: the earliest date the activity can end
- *Late Finish*: the latest date the activity can end and still allow the project to be completed on time

Project management software is commonly used for critical path calculations. Once you enter the activity durations and preceding activities, the program determines the critical path and the early start, early finish, late start, and late finish dates. This saves significant time creating the original schedule and subsequent reschedules. The following sections explain how these values are calculated manually in a two-step process with a forward pass and a backward pass.

Forward Pass

A forward pass calculates the *early start* and *early finish*, which are the earliest points in time an activity can start and finish, respectively. To compute these figures, start from the left side (the project start) of a network diagram and continue to ask yourself, as you proceed incrementally to the right, ''What is the earliest time I can start and finish an activity?'' Using Figure 5-7, follow these four steps:

1. Start the project on the beginning of day zero. Therefore, the earliest time the first activity (WP 1.1) can start is day zero.
2. Add the duration of that activity to the early start to determine the earliest time the activity can finish (WP 1.1 has a duration of five days; therefore, the early finish is the beginning of day five).

$$\text{Start} + \text{Duration} = \text{Finish}$$

3. The *early start* for WP 1.2, WP 1.3, and WP 1.5 is, therefore, the beginning of day five. Repeat the above process for each of those work packages. Proceed from left to right.

4. Work package 1.9 must wait for WP 1.5, WP 1.7, and WP 1.8 to complete before it can start. The earliest time WP 1.9 can start is day twenty-two.

Backward Pass

Determining *late start* and *late finish* is done in exactly the opposite way as was done to determine early start and early finish. Instead of proceeding from left to right, we proceed from right to left. And instead of asking, ''What is the earliest time we can start the activity?'' we ask, ''What is the latest time we can finish the activity without delaying the project?'' Follow these five steps to conduct a backward pass:

1. Start at the end of the project. Since WP 1.9 must be complete to end the project, we ask, ''What is the latest time we can finish WP 1.9 without delaying the project?'' The answer is day twenty-seven—the end date of the project.
2. Since we've determined when the work package will end, we compute the late start by subtracting the duration. For WP 1.9:

$$27 - 5 = 22$$

3. Continuing from right to left, work packages 1.5, 1.7, and 1.8 must finish before WP 1.9 can start. Therefore we ask, ''What is the latest time we can finish these WPs without delaying WP 1.9?'' The answer is day twenty-two. Therefore, the *late finish* for these work packages is day twenty-two.

4. Continue the same process moving right to left for work packages 1.4, 1.2, 1.6, and 1.3.
5. WP 1.1 must complete before WP 1.2, WP 1.3, and WP 1.5 can start. The latest time that WP 1.1 can finish, therefore, is the earliest late-start time of these three work packages. Therefore, WP 1.1 must complete by day five (see WP 1.3). The late start for WP 1.1 is then computed to be day zero.

Project Float

The term *float* (also known as *slack*) refers to the amount of time an activity can slip without affecting the project end date. Mathematically, it is the difference between the early finish and late finish. For activities on the critical path, the early and late start (and early and late finish) are the same, and therefore they have zero float. *Free float* is the amount of time an activity can be delayed without affecting any successor.

CHAPTER

–6–

ESTIMATING WORK

At this point, you have completed several key parts of project planning. You defined and bounded project scope, selected the best strategy or approach to meet project objectives, crafted a complete work breakdown structure, listed intermediate and final deliverables of the project, and built a network diagram that described the preferred sequence in which work packages would be performed. Now we can address estimating—an effort to determine the time, cost, and effort needed to accomplish each work package in the WBS.

Estimating is a form of prediction. Predictions rest on assumptions and have associated probabilities of coming true. All estimates have some confidence and risk associated with them. Consequently, the estimating experience has associated motivational and psychological issues.

This chapter addresses ways to estimate work. By the end of this chapter, you will be better able to estimate the duration of project activities, estimate labor content for project activities, price out a WBS, and complete an estimate network.

Work Breakdown Structure

The work breakdown structure is the foundation for estimating. There are certain parts of project planning that are best done from the top down. Building a new WBS is typically handled this way. Functional decomposition progressively gets to smaller and smaller pieces of work until, at last, we get to work packages or activities that are small in size, unique in terms of organizational responsibility, and consumers of time, resources, and cost. These work packages are the basis for estimating.

Work package estimates are then rolled up or summarized to create project master plans for schedule, resource usage, and costs. The WBS elements are then used to monitor and control work, to detect variances from the approved plan, to initiate corrective actions, and to serve as a basis for lessons learned during the closure process.

Estimate Parameters

Estimates are predictions for three plan parameters:

1. *Time:* How long it will take to accomplish the work in terms of hours, days, weeks, or months

2. *Resources:* How many units of labor, equipment, or supplies are likely to be used
3. *Cost:* How much each work package will cost and how much the entire project will cost

Duration estimates are plugged into the network diagram to create the project's master schedule and critical path. As we shall in Chapter 7, this schedule can be shown as a Gantt chart, a network diagram, or a spreadsheet.

The resources required for each work package are estimated and applied to the schedule. This is called *resource allocation* or *resource distribution*. If imbalances exist—usually because demand exceeds supply or because requirements exceed capacity—then the process selectively repeats itself. This iteration is called *resource smoothing*. The net effect is that, in a resource-limited environment, we arrive at a reasoned solution that allocates the right people with the right skills to the right activities at the right time.

The project budget is the WBS expressed in financial terms. In an ideal world, we create a plan-driven budget, not a budget-driven plan. As the planning process goes on, management has several opportunities to fine-tune or to calibrate the relationships among time, cost, and scope. Clearly, the key to this recalibration is the accuracy and usefulness of the estimates for each work package. The entire process is illustrated in Figure 6-1.

Estimating Methods

The four basic methods for estimating activities are analogous, parametric, bottom-up, and simulation.

Figure 6-1. Estimating and the Project Planning Process.

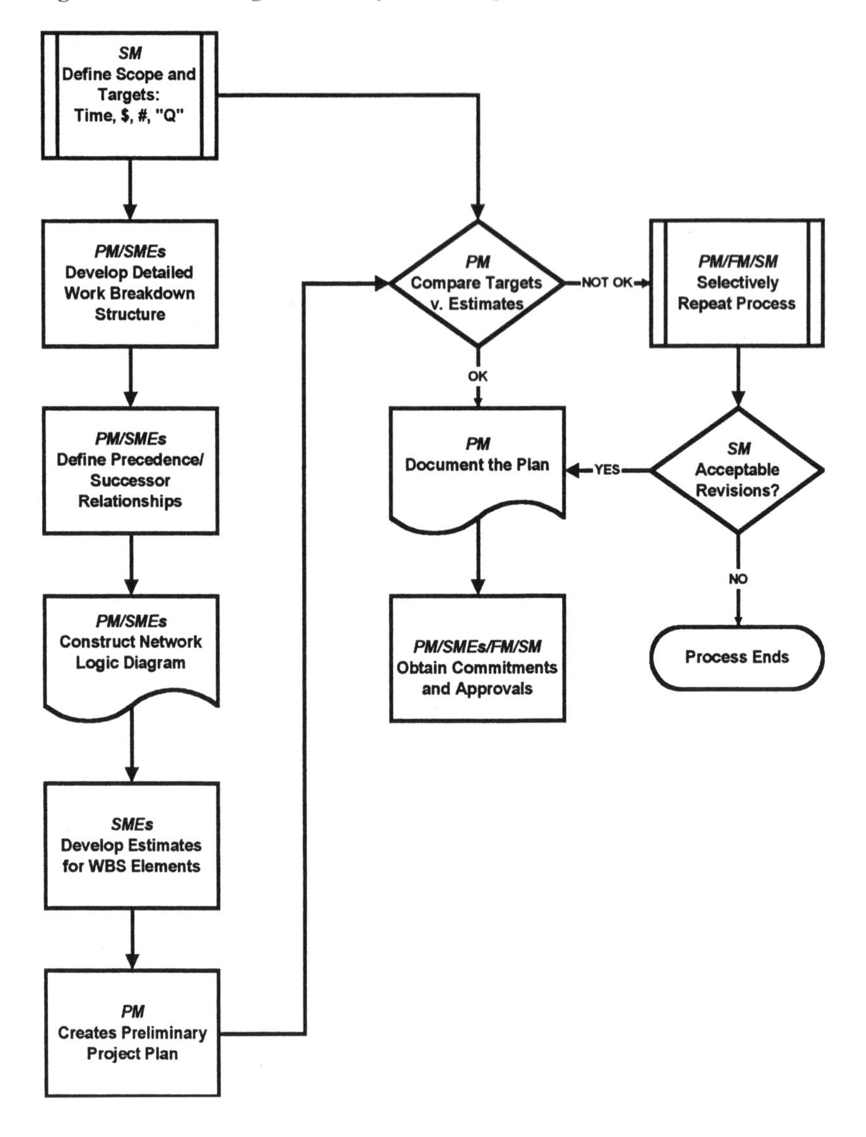

Analogous Approach

This approach uses the actual costs and durations of previous, similar projects as the basis for estimating the current project. It uses historical information from the organization as well as industry standards. It is also called a *top-down* estimate, because it relies on information from the top row of activities of the work breakdown structure. It can be used to estimate projects with a limited amount of detailed information. For example, a project to implement a new accounts payable process in one company may be estimated by reference to a similar accounts payable process that was recently implemented in another company. Such an analogous approach is generally less costly than other approaches, but is also generally less accurate.

Parametric Modeling

Parametric modeling uses mathematical parameters to predict project costs. An example is residential home construction that is often estimated using a certain dollar amount per square foot of floor space. Complex examples can be found in the software development industry where one model uses thirteen separate adjustment factors, each of which has five to seven points. The cost and accuracy of parametric estimates vary widely.

Bottom-Up Estimate

This approach estimates the cost and duration of the individual work packages from the bottom row of activities of the work breakdown structure, then totals the amounts up each row until reaching an estimate for the total project.

This approach can produce a more accurate estimate, but at a higher cost.

Simulation

In this approach, a computer calculates multiple costs or durations with different sets of assumptions. The most common is the Monte Carlo method, in which a range of probable results is defined for each activity and used to calculate a range of probable results for the total project. Simulation can provide a more accurate estimate and is principally used on large or complex projects.

Guidelines for Estimating

Estimators routinely rely on the following five guidelines to create estimates that are realistic and achievable: the ownership of estimates rule, the level of detail rule, the distribution of estimates rule, the human productivity rule, and the time/cost/resource trade-off rule.

Ownership of Estimates Rule

The ownership of estimates rule says that those answerable for specific results should make (or at least participate and review) the estimates for which they will thereafter be held accountable. The reason for this rule is twofold:

1. Subject matter experts (or practitioners) know more about specific work packages than the project manager does. If the project manager is skeptical about the initial estimates received, she should respect the expertise of others.

2. An estimate dictated to a functional group or department from higher up generates little or no loyalty to the estimate by those who perform the work. A project manager who dictates an estimate (for example, "You'll have to get this done by the fifteenth of next month and your budget is $6,500.") sets everyone up to fail.

When the functional or resource manager cannot predict which employee will be assigned to the work package, then she should assume average performance and productivity of the work group.

Level of Detail Rule

The level of detail rule suggests that the smaller the unit of work being estimated, the better the estimate is likely to be. To answer the question "How much will the new system cost?" on the first day of a project is folly. A better question might be "How much time, effort, and money will be required to determine the feasibility of system Q?" Still better is the estimating question "How many labor hours will be required to create four to six data entry/capture screens for an order entry system?" What made the estimating questions progressively better was that the questions dealt in progressive detail within a work breakdown system.

Distribution of Estimates Rule

The third rule of estimating is the distribution of estimates rule. This rule holds that for any work package the best estimate has the same likelihood of being early or late, over or under. The easiest way to grasp this rule is shown graphically in Figure 6-2. This figure has three curves or distribution patterns reflecting three kinds of estimators.

The middle curve shows a pattern of estimates against actual results achieved with two important characteristics. First, the curve shows little variance (0 ± 1); second, it has no left or right skew. In short, what was estimated was what routinely occurred.

The curve on the left of the graph is that of the worst-case estimator. On a regular basis, this estimator presents estimates (whether for time, resources, or costs) for a work

Figure 6-2. The Distribution of Estimates.

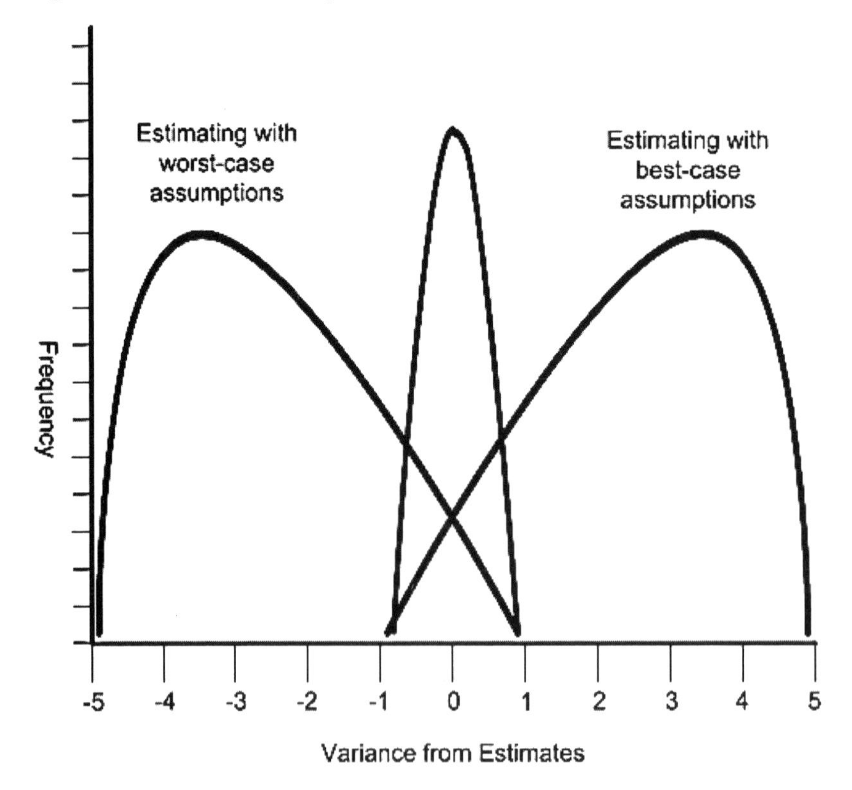

package and then routinely beats the estimate (that is, the work package is done substantially earlier or for less money). Initially, this seems to be a positive outcome. Upon reflection, however, it has several genuine flaws:

- If the estimates are needed to attract new business, none will materialize because the prospective customer sees too high a price or bears too great a share of the risk.
- Enterprise resources were committed, based on the estimates, that could have been used elsewhere.
- The enterprise may incur unforeseen costs for inventory storage, product obsolescence, or decay and malfunction.

Estimators in this field need coaching to help them learn to take prudent risks when asked to estimate.

The curve on the right of the graph represents the overly optimistic estimator who looks at life through rose-colored glasses. Each work package is estimated on assumptions of a best-case scenario. Regrettably, this type of estimator makes promises that do not materialize because risks were neither identified nor quantified. The net result is the distribution pattern where activities are completed later than they should be, use more resource units than were planned, and cost more than the approved budget. The net effect is that the anticipated benefit streams, regardless of how they are calculated, do not materialize, and the customer is disappointed in the project's return on investment.

We can rephrase the distribution of estimates rule in the

following way: (1) do not politicize estimates to make your supervisor, customer, or client happy; (2) tell the truth; (3) negotiate requirements first and budgets second; and (4) estimates should be neither too lean nor too heavy.

Human Productivity Rule

The fourth estimating rule, the human productivity rule, states that people cannot be expected to perform their activities with uniform production over a business day. When providing an estimate for a work package, take into account the items shown in Figure 6-3. This table begins with an assumption of one subject matter expert working eight hours a day for a five-day week. If we further assume an hourly cost of $75, then line one of the table becomes the base estimate for the activity. Eroding productivity will be project loss factors and rework (lines two and three). In addition, there will be further erosion due to vacations, sick leave, holidays, and so on. The net effect is that real work is done in roughly 1,768 hours per year, rather than the 2,080 hours of available time in a year.

Time/Cost/Resource Trade-Off Rule

The final estimating rule recognizes a trade-off among time, cost, and resource hours needed for a work package. The relationship is illustrated in Figure 6-4.

Figure 6-3. Factors That Erode Productivity.

Productivity Factor	Hours	Cost per Hour	Labor Cost	Duration
Base Estimate	40	$75	$3,000	5.00 days
Project Loss Factor (@15% of base)	6	75	450	.75
Rework/Debug Factor (@10% of base)	4	75	300	.50
Subtotal (for direct costing)	50	75	3,750	6.25
Nonproject Loss Factor (@15% of base)	6	—	—	.75
Grand total for scheduling	56	—	—	7.00

Figure 6-4. Time/Cost/Resource Trade-Off Curve.

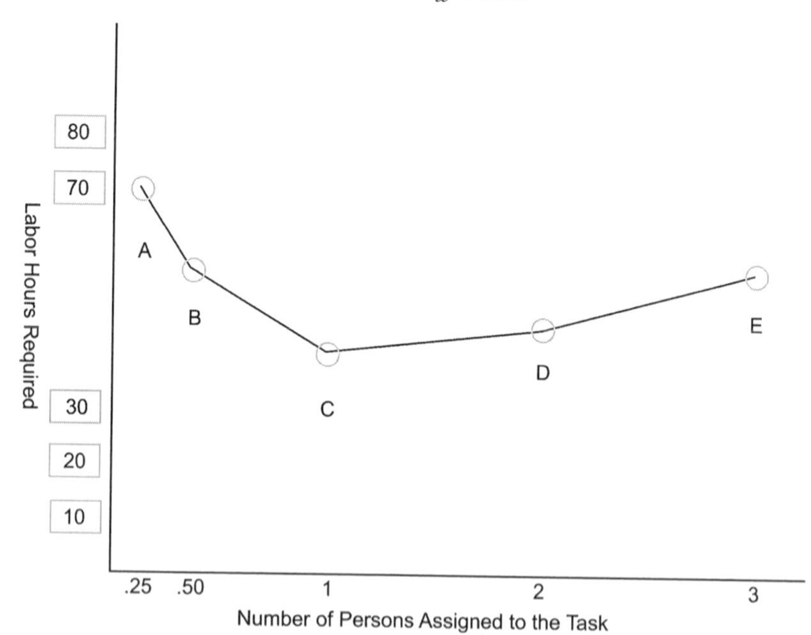

Assume an activity could be done by one practitioner working without interruption over the course of a week. The cost per hour for this expert is $75. The estimate for this work package becomes:

Time = 5 days
Labor content = 40 hours
Labor cost = $3,000

This is reflected as point *C* in the figure that follows. If we must add another expert to the activity, then we discover at point *D* in the drawing that total time may be compressed, but labor hours and costs increase because of communication that must occur. Point *E* carries this example further to show what is likely to happen when management assigns three staff members to perform an activity that could most efficiently be done by a single worker without interruption. Points *A* and *B* indicate what happens when staff members are assigned to multiple activities simultaneously—they become increasingly less productive with each newly assigned activity. The empirical results of the trade-off are shown in Figure 6-5.

Estimates Should Consider Risks

The time, cost, and resource estimates for a work package should reflect the degree of risk associated with that activity. If an activity is well understood, familiar to practitioners, routinely done, and frequently recalibrated to reflect best practices, then the estimate for the work package should consider a low-risk factor. The distribution pattern of a low-risk item (see Figure 6-6) is spiked at or near variance of zero, with neither left nor right skew. Activities with this low risk level are often found in estimating handbooks or guidelines for auto repairs and construction.

If the work package is somewhat well understood but still has important variables that could influence its out-

Figure 6-5. Time/Cost/Resource Trade-Off Data Points.

Data Points	Staffing Pattern (Simplified)	Task Duration	Labor Hours Needed	Labor Cost (@ $75/hour)
A	0.25 (two hours/day)	35.00 days	70.00	5,250
B	0.50 (four hours/day)	14.00 days	56.00	4,200
C	1.00 (8 hours/day)	5.00 days	40.00	3,000
D	2.00 (16 hours/day)	2.75 days	44.00	3,300
E	3.00 (24 hours/day)	2.33 days	56.00	4,200

Figure 6-6. Distribution Pattern of a Low-Risk Item.

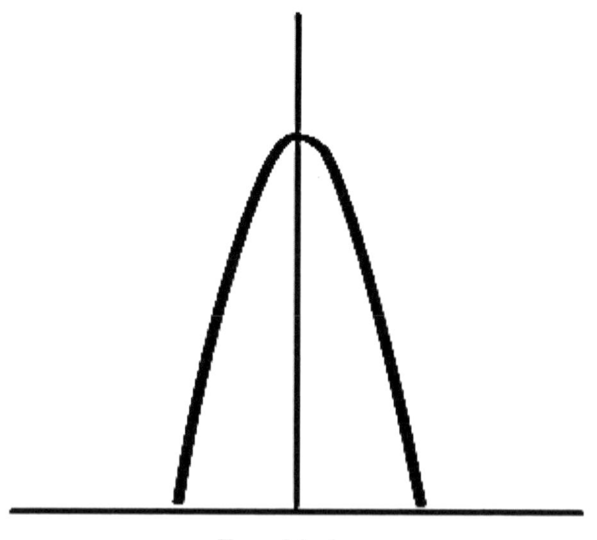

come, then you should use a normal distribution as the underlying model for estimating. This distribution is illustrated in Figure 6-7, along with its indications for three standard deviations from the mean. This diagram shows that 95 times out of 100 the predicted outcome or estimate occurs within two standard deviations of the (arithmetic) mean. The most likely outcome takes up four estimating zones in the curve. Best-case and worst-case outcomes occur far less frequently—roughly once in every 20 instances.

This distribution gives rise to the program evaluation and review technique (PERT), which is a weighted-average estimating equation. This equation requires you to gather three estimates: a most likely estimate (given what you expect to happen), an optimistic estimate (if everything goes

Figure 6-7. Normal Distribution Curve.

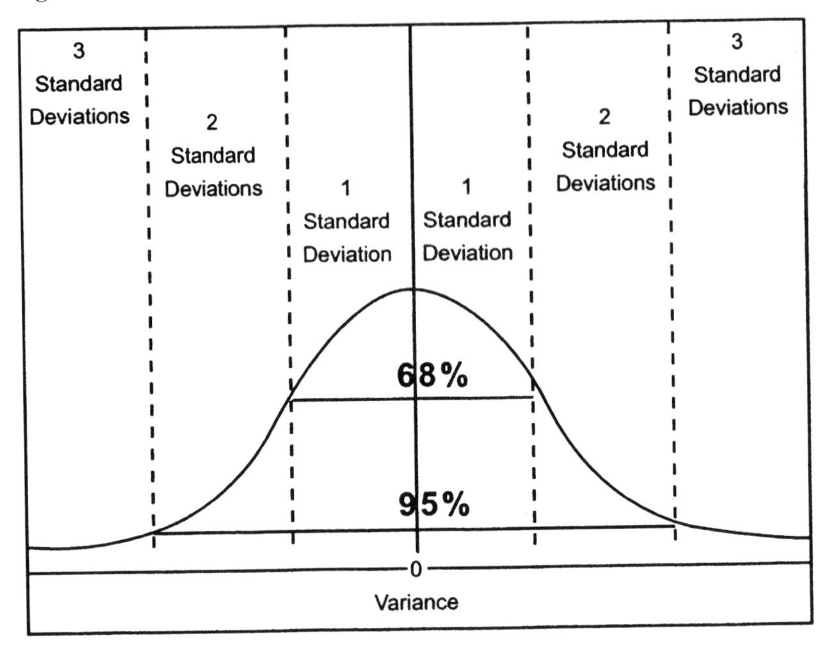

very well), and a pessimistic estimate (if things go poorly). You then combine the three estimates to calculate the average expected duration or cost for the activity, using the following formula:

$$\text{estimated time} = \frac{\text{optimistic} + (4 \times \text{most likely}) + \text{pessimistic}}{6}$$

This weighted estimate accounts for the uncertainty and variability inherent in project work and provides a risk-adjusted estimate. It works equally well for both time and cost estimates.

Effort-Driven vs. Duration-Driven Estimates

So far in this chapter we have made the following points:

- The work breakdown structure is the foundation for estimating because it is developed top-down in terms of decomposition and bottom-up in terms of estimating.
- Each work package has three estimates associated with it: time, asset and resource usage, and cost.
- Realistic and achievable estimates tend to follow five guidelines.
- Estimating is an iterative process, selectively retracing appropriate steps to achieve balance between supply and demand, and between capacity and requirements.
- Estimates are predictions and have varying degrees of confidence associated with them. Risk elements play a key role in estimating.

There is one final point to be made. Work packages may be either duration-based or effort-based.

Duration-based activities require a fixed duration for completion. Examples include laboratory experiments to grow specific tumors in mice, backing up a file (of known size, buffers, and read/write speeds), or auto travel. Adding staff does not compress the schedule but may add considerably to labor costs.

Effort-based activities may be compressed in duration by adding staff. The schedule may be compressed, but costs and risks may rise.

Duration-based and effort-based activity distinction

has practical applications. If activities are on the project's critical path, then estimators must be certain that such an activity has a duration-based estimate. If an activity has significant slack or float, then perhaps an effort-based estimate is appropriate. This type of estimate may permit deployment of entry-level staff or of newer associates. If the schedule slips, the results may not be catastrophic.

Estimates Are Predictions

Your projects—regardless of type, topic, or industry—must meet expectations. Increasingly, you are asked to create aggressive schedules with limited or untested resources. You are pressured to prepare or accept estimates that are driven by political rather than technical considerations. As a result, you should be aware of estimating tools that may help you and your team. For the most part, these tools stem from information systems and information technology projects. Nonetheless, you can apply them to almost any project after some modification and fine-tuning.

Life-Cycle Distribution

Certain projects follow predictable patterns that tell us what part of a project is spent on a particular phase or stage of work. For example, some industries use a 1 × 10 × 10 rule. For every dollar spent in conceptual effort, then ten dollars will be spent in product design and engineering. In turn, each hour or dollar devoted to design and engineering will generate another ten hours in programming, construction, fabrication, or assembly.

One popular notion in the information systems community is expressed in Figure 6-8. Project life-cycle stages are in column one and rough assessments of project complexity are in the subsequent columns.

The key points from this table are:

- ❑ The more complex the system, the greater the need for artful and complete definition of scope and requirements.
- ❑ If the assignment is fairly simple and self-contained, then proportionately more effort is spent doing the work than in planning it.

Variance Factors

A second and related method of estimating presumes a reliable database with estimates for specific work packages. Traditionally, this database is built with information from prior projects on the actual time, cost, and labor used to

Figure 6-8. Distribution of Effort in an IS Project.

Life-Cycle Stages	Simple	Moderate	Complex
Feasibility Study	1%-2%	2%-4%	3%-5%
Requirements Definition	8-10	10-15	15-20
Systems Specifications	10-15	12-18	15-20
Systems Design	12-15	15-18	18-25
Program Development	30-40	25-30	20-25
System Testing	10-15	12-18	15-20
Implementation	5-10	8-12	10-15

reach the end of the activity. The current project is then compared against the preexisting base. If the new project is easier to do than the standard, the estimates are revised downward. If the new project is more complex than the standard, the estimates are revised upward. The following are some factors that may influence estimates:

- System size and complexity
- Extent of innovation required
- Number of sites where work is to be performed; cultural issues
- Prior experience of team members; ergonomic factors
- Capacity and throughput rates of machinery
- Quality definitions (from clients, customers, or government)
- Industry codes, conventions, and standards
- Material properties, composition, physical, and chemical reactions

Quality of the Estimate

The quality of an estimate should improve over time. Sometimes, estimates made at the beginning of a project are predicated on a whim ("Whatever it takes to win the job") or on political correctness ("The boss says we have $125,000 in the budget"). None of these "methods" reflect evidence, a well-thought-out work breakdown structure, or an analysis of risk and uncertainty.

Figure 6-9. Estimating Accuracy Over Time.

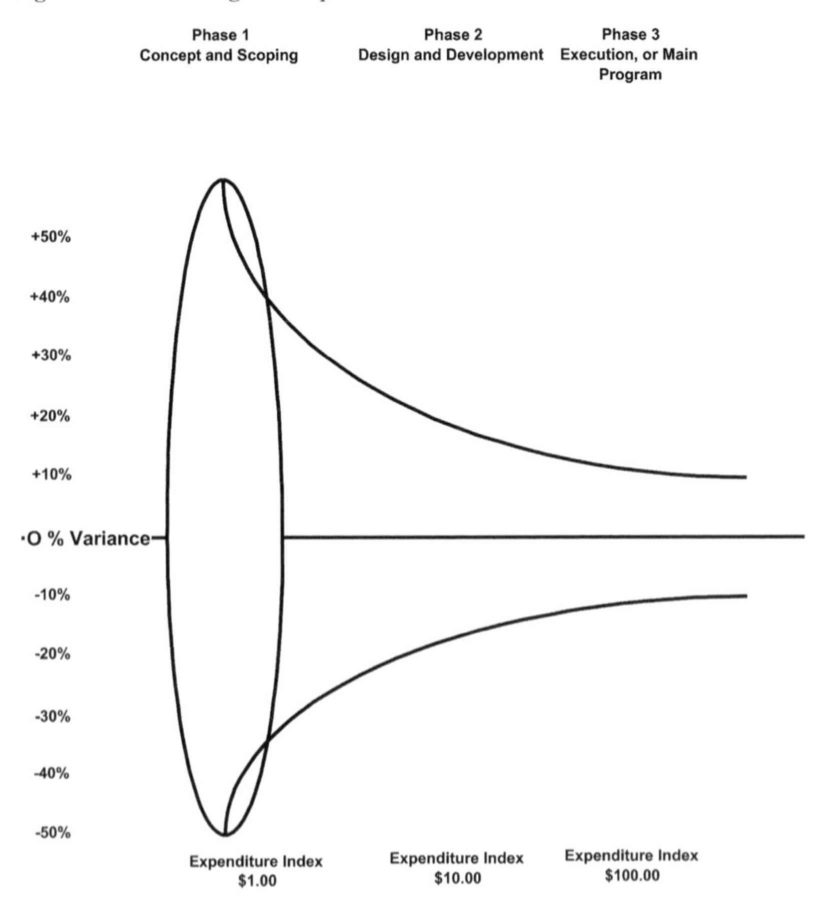

Many organizations address this fact by adopting the idea of an estimating funnel. The two main ideas behind this funnel, illustrated in Figure 6-9, are these: (1) estimates get better the more we know about the work to be done and the metrics associated with the project's goal, and (2) it is acceptable to have different levels of confidence for estimates at various points in the project.

For example, one engineering and construction company uses these guidelines:

> Conceptual phase of the project can be estimated at + 50%
> Preliminary engineering phase + 25%
> Detailed engineering phase + 10%
> Construction phase + 5–7%

Part III

PUTTING IT TOGETHER

CHAPTER

–7–

Producing a Project Plan

In Chapters 1 through 6, you completed several steps related to project initiation and planning. You defined project scope, developed an appropriate and tailored work breakdown structure, sequenced the work packages in a network logic diagram, and obtained estimates from subject matter experts. This chapter will explain how to create and document an integrated project plan, communicate the plan to others, and secure necessary commitments and approvals. The final result of the planning process is a management decision on whether to proceed with the execution of the project.

Components of a Project Plan

An integrated project plan is a set of eight separate but linked documents that display scope, the activity schedule, the planned distribution and allocation of assets and resources, the project cost or budget, an index or list of key deliverables, organizational roles and responsibilities, a risk management plan, and a communication plan.

The scope document defines the purpose and rationale of the project. It describes, at a fairly high level, the results to be achieved, the products and services to be delivered, and the links between your goals and the broader goals of the enterprise. This document may also be called a business case or a project prospectus.

The schedule shows the start and end dates of work packages and the anticipated duration for each work item. Typically, the schedule plan also shows the roll-up of all work items to indicate total duration. The schedule plan must also reflect the logical dependencies among work packages so that the sequence of work can be understood and displayed.

The resource utilization plan displays the distribution of people, equipment, material, supplies, and other assets. Ideally, this distribution is tied to specific work packages; often, however, this distribution appears only at fairly high levels in the work breakdown structure.

The cost plan or budget is the financial expression of the work breakdown structure. The cost plan or budget depicts the costs likely to be committed, accrued, or obligated by work package for each interval in the schedule. In some organizations, the cost plan is balanced against a revenue projection plan to calculate net cash flows for the performing organization.

The milestone plan indicates the key deliverables that arise during the life of the project, their due dates, the organization or department responsible for producing them, and the organization or department expecting their receipt as a condition of starting its own work.

The organization plan establishes the relationships between work packages and organization components. The purpose of the organization plan is to ensure that every work package has an owner or champion, that no activity is orphaned, and that complex and subtle relationships among players are well understood.

The risk management plan, evolving throughout the planning process, incorporates (1) risk identification; (2) qualitative and quantitative assessments; (3) strategies for prevention, detection, and mitigation of loss; and (4) recovery and restoration of functions.

The communication plan describes how the project manager will keep information flowing during the project. This plan should describe meetings and reports as well as the frequency and content of reports sent to senior management, stakeholders, and the client. It should also describe the frequency and agenda for regular and exception meetings, such as team status meetings and senior management project reviews.

Management may require other items in a project plan. Some executives require a formal risk management component; others look for detailed financial analyses. Some executives look for acceptance-test plans, and others look for explicit linkages between technology and organizational goals. Still others want written opinions from legal counsel, authorizations and permits from regulatory bodies or clients, and so on.

Before you submit your integrated project plan, review it carefully with your planning team and get the necessary commitments from resource owners to provide the staff and other assets you will need. The plan you submit will need the appropriate approvals and authorizations before you proceed.

An easy way to imagine selected parts of an integrated project plan is to think of a spreadsheet. Columns represent units of time, such as hours, days, weeks, or months. Rows are elements of the work breakdown structure. The cells in the table will then be filled with bars, labor hours, costs, or deliverables.

In this view, cells in a schedule plan show work packages versus units of time. Cells in a resource plan show the number of resource units required by work package and time frame. Cells in a cost plan show the cost per period for each work package. For both the resource and cost plans, we can summarize across a row to get the work package total; alternatively, we can summarize down each column to get aggregate demand per unit of time.

Conceptually, each plan could be an overlay of the others. Thus, people cannot be assigned to work packages when the schedule indicates that no work is to be performed; costs cannot accrue when work is not being performed.

Schedule Plan

The schedule plan shows specific work packages with estimates for time and sequence. You can build your schedule plan using these three elements:

1. Work package descriptions from the work breakdown structure (see Chapter 4)
2. Dependency relationships from the network diagram (see Chapter 5)
3. Duration estimates (see Chapter 6)

You can display your project's schedule in various ways:

- ❑ Bar or Gantt charts (with or without dependencies shown)
- ❑ Network diagrams (with or without durations displayed)
- ❑ Spreadsheets (usually customized to meet specific needs of an enterprise or a project)

Figure 7-1 shows a generic critical path bar chart. Please review the chart and then answer the following questions:

- ❑ Which activities are on the critical path?
- ❑ How do you know?
- ❑ What type(s) of dependency relationship(s) appear(s) in the drawing?
- ❑ What must be done before work package eight can begin?
- ❑ What happens if work package nine starts two weeks after its early start date?
- ❑ If work package nine is done, but work package eleven is not, what (if anything) happens to the start of work package twelve?

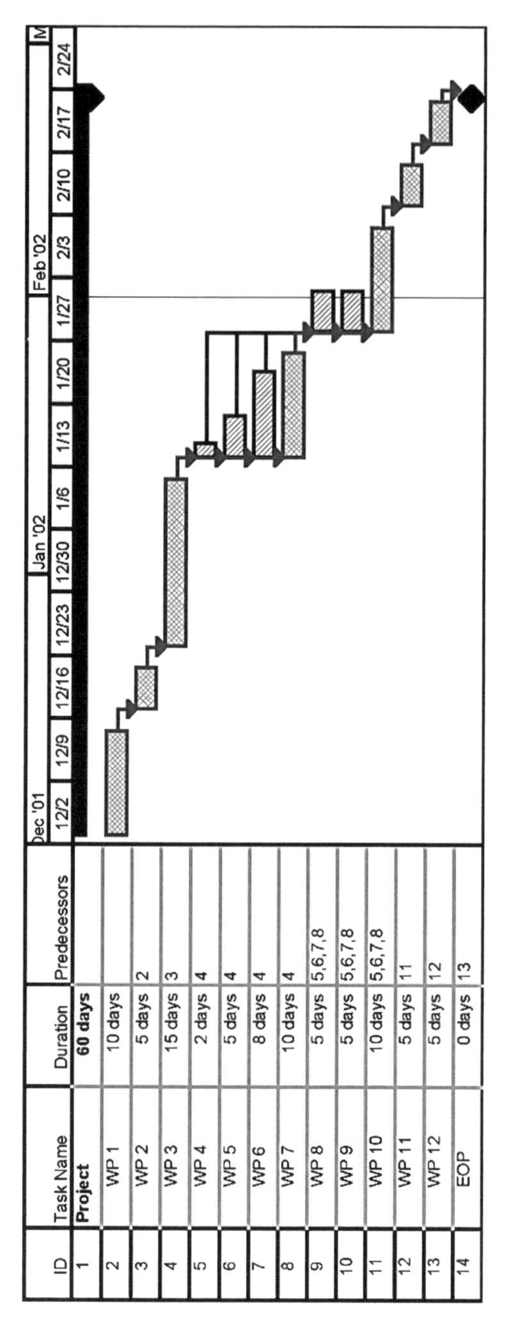

ID	Task Name	Duration	Predecessors
1	**Project**	**60 days**	
2	WP 1	10 days	
3	WP 2	5 days	2
4	WP 3	15 days	3
5	WP 4	2 days	4
6	WP 5	5 days	4
7	WP 6	8 days	4
8	WP 7	10 days	4
9	WP 8	5 days	5,6,7,8
10	WP 9	5 days	5,6,7,8
11	WP 10	10 days	5,6,7,8
12	WP 11	5 days	11
13	WP 12	5 days	12
14	EOP	0 days	13

Figure 7-1. Illustrative Critical Path Bar Chart.

- ❑ What is the immediate predecessor for work package three? For work package eleven?
- ❑ If work packages eight and nine require the same person, what is likely to happen and why?

The information in this Gantt chart could also be transformed and presented as a network diagram or as a table (see Figure 7-2). As you review the table, remember that:

(Late Finish) − (Early Finish) = Float

A more complex example of project schedule information, using the example we introduced earlier, appears in Figure 7-3. You can construct the project schedule—either manually or with almost any automated scheduling tool—if you keep the conceptual equation in mind:

Work Packages + Dependency Relationships + Durations = Schedule

Resource and Budget Plans

Resource and budget plans are linked to project schedules. After a preliminary project schedule is developed, the project planning team "populates" each work package with a mix of people, materials, equipment and supplies, trips, and so on. The spreadsheet metaphor reappears as the project manager guides the planning team through the steps shown in Figure 7-4 on page 134.

Let us look at the essential parts of a resource plan. The first thing we need to do is create an inventory of people

Figure 7-2. Project Schedule as a Table.

ID	Task Name	Duration	Predecessors	Early Start	Early Finish	Late Start	Late Finish	Total Slack
1	**Project**	**60 days**		**Mon 12/3/01**	**Fri 2/22/02**	**Mon 12/3/01**	**Fri 2/22/02**	**0 days**
2	WP 1	10 days		Mon 12/3/01	Fri 12/14/01	Mon 12/3/01	Fri 12/14/01	0 days
3	WP 2	5 days	2	Mon 12/17/01	Fri 12/21/01	Mon 12/17/01	Fri 12/21/01	0 days
4	WP 3	15 days	3	Mon 12/24/01	Fri 1/18/02	Mon 12/24/01	Fri 1/18/02	0 days
5	WP 4	2 days	4	Mon 1/21/02	Tue 1/22/02	Thu 1/31/02	Fri 2/1/02	8 days
6	WP 5	5 days	4	Mon 1/21/02	Fri 1/25/02	Mon 1/28/02	Fri 2/1/02	5 days
7	WP 6	8 days	4	Mon 1/21/02	Wed 1/30/02	Wed 1/23/02	Fri 2/1/02	2 days
8	WP 7	10 days	4	Mon 1/21/02	Fri 2/1/02	Mon 1/21/02	Fri 2/1/02	0 days
9	WP 8	5 days	5,6,7,8	Mon 2/4/02	Fri 2/8/02	Mon 2/18/02	Fri 2/22/02	10 days
10	WP 9	5 days	5,6,7,8	Mon 2/4/02	Fri 2/8/02	Mon 2/18/02	Fri 2/22/02	10 days
11	WP 10	10 days	5,6,7,8	Mon 2/4/02	Fri 2/15/02	Mon 2/4/02	Fri 2/15/02	0 days
12	WP 11	5 days	11	Mon 2/18/02	Fri 2/22/02	Mon 2/18/02	Fri 2/22/02	0 days
13	EOP	0 days	12	Fri 2/22/02	Fri 2/22/02	Fri 2/22/02	Fri 2/22/02	0 days

Figure 7-3. Project Work Breakdown Structure (with Durations and Dependencies).

ID	Task Name	Duration	Predecessors
1	**AMA Example: Feasibility Study Template**	**16 days**	
2	**Initial Problem Definition/Opportunity Analysis**	**2.5 days**	
3	Receive Charter from Initiation Process; Review	0.5 days	
4	Confirm Project Targets for Time, Cost and Requirements	0.5 days	3
5	Create Cross-Functional Team for this Phase of the Project	1 day	4
6	Determine Current Status of Project and/or Problem	0.5 days	5
7	**Collect Relevant Information**	**6 days**	**6**
8	**Identify Direct Sources of Evidence and Information**	**6 days**	**5**
9	Schedule and Conduct Site Visit(s) and Inspections	3 days	5
10	Schedule and Conduct Interviews	3 days	9
11	Schedule and Conduct Verification Tests	1 day	9
12	Obtain Other Information TBD	1 day	9
13	**Identify Indirect Sources of Evidence and Information**	**1.5 days**	**6**
14	Collect and Review Relevant Operational Documentation	1.5 days	6
15	Collect and Review Organizational and Administrative Data	1 day	6
16	Collect and Review Legal and Contractual Data	0.5 days	6
17	Collect and Review Economic, Financial,and Performance Data	1.5 days	6
18	Collect and Review Other Relevant Information TBD	0.5 days	6
19	**Confirm the Problem Definition or Opportunity Analysis**	**2 days**	**8,13**
20	Document the "As Is" Condition	1 day	10,11,12,14,15,16,17,18
21	Document the "To Be" Condition	1 day	10,11,12,14,15,16,17,18
22	Document the "Gap Analysis"	0.5 days	20,21
23	Secure Agreement(s) as to the Problem Definition	0.5 days	22
24	**Develop Alternative Solutions**	**1.5 days**	**23**
25	Develop "Quick Fix" Operational Alternatives	0.5 days	22
26	Develop Mid-Term "Tactical" Alternatives	0.5 days	22
27	Develop Long-Term "Strategic" Alternatives	1 day	22
28	Rule Out Non-Viable Alternatives	0.5 days	25,26,27
29	**Evaluate Viable Alternatives**	**2 days**	**28**
30	**Determine Technical Feasibility, for example**	**0.5 days**	**28**
31	Configuration Integrity: Hardware, Software, Netware	0.25 days	
32	Best Availability Proven Technology; Applicable "Gold Standards"	0.25 days	
33	Conformity with Scientific and Technical Standards	0.5 days	
34	**Determine Operational Feasibility**	**1 day**	**28**
35	Work Flows and Business Processes	0.5 days	
36	Staff and Skill Competencies vs. New Process	0.5 days	
37	Facility and Layout vs. New Process	1 day	
38	Machinery and Equipment vs. New Process	1 day	
39	Organization Structure vs. New Process	1 day	
40	**Determine Economic Feasibility**	**1 day**	**28**
41	**Estimate Costs for Each Alternative**	**1 day**	
42	Estimate 1-time Costs for Design and Development and Deplc	1 day	
43	Estimate Recurring (O&M) Costs for Each Alternative	1 day	
44	**Estimate Benefit Streams for Each Alternative**	**1 day**	
45	Estimate Appropriate Measures of Return, e.g., ROI, NPV, IRI	1 day	
46	Estimate Contribution to Profit	1 day	
47	Estimate Cost Avoidances and Savings	1 day	
48	Estimate Performance and Quality Improvements	1 day	
49	**Determine Compliance with Applicable Laws, Rules, and Regulatior**	**1 day**	**30,34,40**
50	Identify "Controlling Legal Authorities"	1 day	
51	Identify Requirements for Due Diligence	1 day	
52	Assess Each Alternative	1 day	
53	**Prepare Report for Management**	**2 days**	**30,34,40,49**
54	Transmittal Letter; Executive Summary	0.5 days	
55	Purpose and Scope	0.5 days	
56	Approach and Methodology	0.25 days	
57	Findings and Conclusions	2 days	
58	Recommendations and Next Steps	2 days	
59	Appendices and References to Working Papers	2 days	

and their skills. Figure 7-5 is an example with competencies shown on a scale of one to five (with five being the highest level of skill).

Fundamentally, resource plans show the need (or demand) for a person, skill set, or other asset by work package and desired time frame. First, resource demands are applied at the work-package level and then summarized to

Figure 7-4. Planning Steps for Resource Planning and Budgeting.

Who	Does What	Product
PM; PMO	Distribute preliminary schedule to SMEs and FMs	
WP Estimators	Estimate resource/asset requirements per work package	Demand function
SMEs; FMs	Compare demand to supply (requirements vs. capacity)	Analysis
FMs	Identify supply/demand imbalances	Document
FMs; SMEs	Develop alternative solutions	Options
FMs; SMEs	(Re)Allocate resources; redistribution; resource leveling	Revisions
PM; PMO	Modify schedule plan, as required	Revised schedule
PM; PMO	Price out the WBS (based on the revised schedule)	Project budget
PM; SM	Compare revised budget to approved targets	Analysis
PM; CPT	Perform necessary iterations	Iterations
PM; SM	Secure essential commitments and approvals	Approvals

Figure 7-5. Enterprise Skills Inventory.

Staff	R&D	EE	Arch	Hydro	Nuclear	Inst
Fig Newton	5.0	3.0	2.5	3.5		2.5
Upper Volta		3.5		2.0		
Watts Up	3.0	4.0				3.0
Ohm Igosh	3.0	4.0				3.0
Ampere Waist	2.5	3.5		1.5		1.5
Designer Jean	1.5	1.5	3.0	1.0		1.0
Muddy Waters			2.5	3.5		2.5
Newt Reno	2.5				4.0	3.5
Posit Ron					3.5	3.0
Viola Lynn Cello						4.5

the project level. Thereafter, these demands are added to nonproject requirements for a particular resource or person to create the total demand across certain time periods. These resource requirement data can be shown as spreadsheets, histograms, or cumulative curves.

The first requirement is to identify the resources by name or type. Figure 7-6 shows a resource pool available for our illustrative project.

Resources are then assigned to specific work packages, as shown in Figure 7-7.

Finally, we can illustrate the distribution of people to work packages in particular time frames. At this point in the planning process, project management software (typically) alerts us that resource demand exceeds resource supply. This imbalance may be shown in a table (see Figure 7-8 on page 138) or in a histogram.

For resource managers, the cells of the table are critical because they describe the anticipated distribution of people to activities on specific days or weeks. For the project manager, the perimeter cells are critical because they define total demand across all activities, skills, asset types, and time frames. When project and resource managers consider the need or demand for labor hours (or any asset or resource), a convenient way to display this information is a histogram. The next three figures indicate how histograms could be used.

Figure 7-9 on page 139 depicts the need for a systems analyst over a ten-week period (presumably the life of the project). Notice that the plan requires this person to work eighty hours a week in weeks four and five, but only twenty hours in week six.

Figure 7-10 on page 140 is a more complex diagram illustrating the planned distribution of time of one person who is assigned to multiple activities, not all of which are projects.

Figure 7-11 on page 141 indicates which persons are assigned to specific work packages.

Figure 7-6. Resource Table.

ID	❶	Resource Name	Initials	Group	Max. Units	Std. Rate	Ovt. Rate	Cost/Use
1		Fig Newton	F	R&D	100%	$250.00/hr	$0.00/hr	$0.00
2		Upper Volta	U	EE	100%	$150.00/hr	$0.00/hr	$0.00
3		Watts Up	W	EE	100%	$150.00/hr	$0.00/hr	$0.00
4		Ohm Igosh	O	EE	100%	$125.00/hr	$0.00/hr	$0.00
5		Ampere Waist	A	EE	100%	$100.00/hr	$0.00/hr	$0.00
6		Designer Jean	D	Architect	100%	$75.00/hr	$0.00/hr	$0.00
7		Muddy Waters	M	Hydro	100%	$75.00/hr	$0.00/hr	$0.00
8		Newt Reno	N	Nuclear	100%	$125.00/hr	$0.00/hr	$0.00
9		Posit Ron	P	Nuclear	100%	$125.00/hr	$0.00/hr	$0.00
10		Viola Lynn Cello	V	Instrument	100%	$150.00/hr	$0.00/hr	$0.00

Figure 7-7. Resources Assigned to Work Packages.

ID	Resource Names	Task Name	Duration	Predecessors
1		**AMA Example: Feasibility Study Template**	**16 days**	
2		**Initial Problem Definition/Opportunity Analysis**	**2.5 days**	
3	Fig Newton	Receive Charter from Initiation Process; Review	0.5 days	
4	Watts Up	Confirm Project Targets for Time, Cost and Requirements	0.5 days	3
5	Upper Volta	Create Cross-Functional Team for this Phase of the Project	1 day	4
6	Fig Newton	Determine Current Status of Project and/or Problem	0.5 days	5
7		**Collect Relevant Information**	**6 days**	**6**
8		**Identify Direct Sources of Evidence and Information**	**6 days**	**5**
9	Muddy Waters	Schedule and Conduct Site Visit(s) and Inspections	3 days	5
10	Newt Reno	Schedule and Conduct Interviews	3 days	9
11	Fig Newton,Ohm Igosh	Schedule and Conduct Verification Tests	0.5 days	9
12	Posit Ron	Obtain Other Information TBD	1 day	9
13		**Identify Indirect Sources of Evidence and Information**	**1.5 days**	**6**
14	Viola Lynn Cello	Collect and Review Relevant Operational Documentation	1.5 days	6
15	Posit Ron	Collect and Review Organizational and Administrative Data	1 day	6
16		Collect and Review Legal and Contractual Data	0.5 days	6
17		Collect and Review Economic, Financial, and Performance Data	1.5 days	6
18		Collect and Review Other Relevant Information TBD	0.5 days	6
19		**Confirm the Problem Definition or Opportunity Analysis**	**2 days**	**8,13**
20		Document the "As Is" Condition	1 day	10,11,12,14,15,16,17,18
21		Document the "To Be" Condition	1 day	10,11,12,14,15,16,17,18
22		Document the "Gap Analysis"	0.5 days	20,21

Figure 7-8. Resources Assigned to Work Packages (by Day).

ID	ℹ	Resource Name	Work	Details	Sep 2, '01					
					S	S	M	T	W	T
1		Fig Newton	12 hrs	Work			4h		4h	
		Receive Charter	*4 hrs*	Work			4h			
		Determine Currer	*4 hrs*	Work					4h	
		Schedule and Co	*4 hrs*	Work						
2		Upper Volta	8 hrs	Work				8h		
		Create Cross-fun	*8 hrs*	Work				8h		
3		Watts Up	4 hrs	Work			4h			
		Confirm Project T	*4 hrs*	Work			4h			
4		Ohm Igosh	4 hrs	Work						
		Schedule and Co	*4 hrs*	Work						
5		Ampere Waist	0 hrs	Work						
6		Designer Jean	0 hrs	Work						
7		Muddy Waters	24 hrs	Work					4h	8h
		Schedule and Co	*24 hrs*	Work					4h	8h
8		Newt Reno	24 hrs	Work						
		Schedule and Co	*24 hrs*	Work						
9		Posit Ron	16 hrs	Work					4h	4h
		Obtain Other Info	*8 hrs*	Work						
		Collect and Revie	*8 hrs*	Work					4h	4h
10		Viola Lynn Cello	12 hrs	Work					4h	8h
		Collect and Revie	*12 hrs*	Work					4h	8h

Figure 7-9. Resource Histogram.

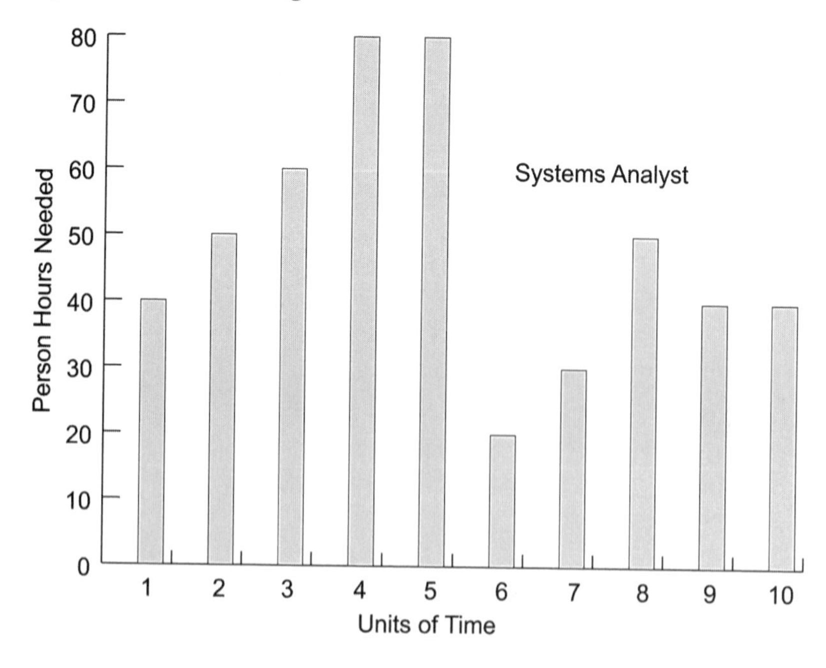

Resource Imbalance

Resource imbalance is a central issue for project and resource managers. A recurring problem is that demand is often greater than supply (or requirements exceed capacity) for people, supplies, and equipment. This imbalance may arise in particular time frames or for particular work packages. This imbalance may be acute or chronic. All solutions require negotiating skills. The following are some actions that can be taken to alleviate the problem:

- Move activities using float, either in this project or in another project. You could also defer other nonproject work.

Figure 7-10. Distribution of a Single Resource Across Work Items.

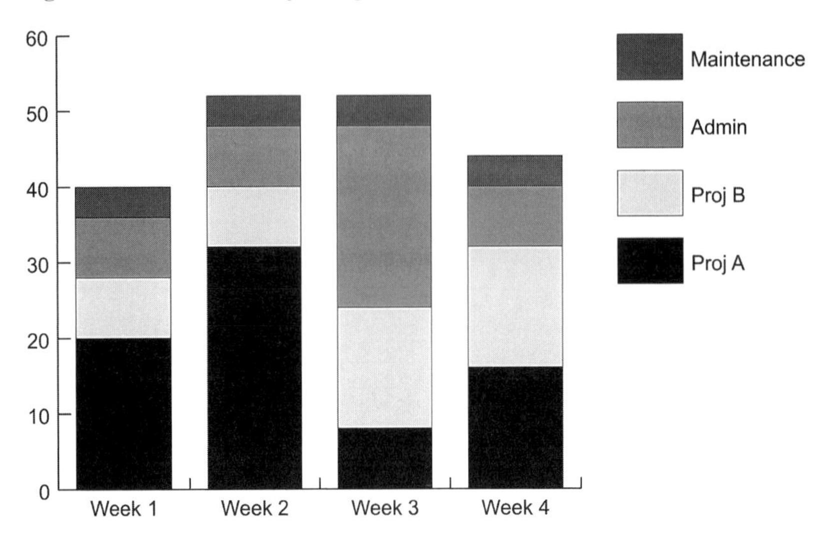

- ❑ Adjust the time/cost/resource trade-off curve. Add people to compress time. Use your best people on high-risk activities. Assign fewer activities per person.
- ❑ Use overtime. Consider employees who are not compensated for overtime and instead grant them compensatory time for the overtime worked.
- ❑ Take measures to improve productivity.
- ❑ Acquire temporary help. Buy skills and deliverables. Assign nonproject personnel to the project.
- ❑ Increase staff, either regular or temporary, full-time or part-time.
- ❑ Use special, one-time incentives. These could be financial rewards or other motivators.
- ❑ Utilize resource-constrained schedules.
- ❑ Change precedence relationships. For example, use lead or lag relationships instead of pure finish-to-start relationships.

Figure 7-11. Distribution of Labor by Staff and Work Packages.

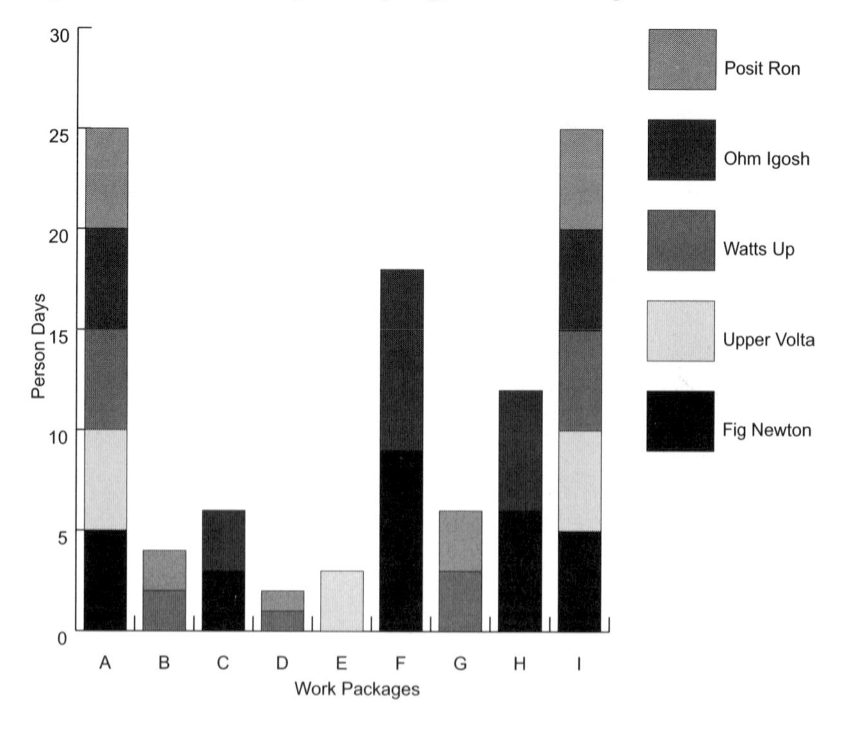

- ❑ Review estimates to see if time or cost savings are possible.
- ❑ Review and revise definitions and metrics for end-item quality.
- ❑ Be careful when using automated resource leveling in project management software.
- ❑ Reprioritize the project inventory.

Project Cost Plan

Another key document in the integrated project plan is the cost plan or project budget. Each organization has its own forms and procedures for displaying and analyzing project cost information. These forms tend to share common characteristics:

- The total project budget is the sum of work package estimates plus financial contingencies.
- Committed costs (also known as obligated or accrued costs) are incurred over periods of time. Some work packages could have these costs applied at the beginning of the activity ("front-end loaded") or at the end of the activity ("back-end loaded"). Alternatively, you may have these costs prorated over the activity's time.
- As a general rule, costs cannot be incurred when work is not being performed.

The net result is another spreadsheet, as illustrated in Figure 7-12. Costs are allocated to each work package by type of cost and by period of time. The cost plan prices out the work breakdown structure, considering costs by type, by time, and by activity. Include both direct and indirect costs. The plan should also reflect commitments and obligations, cash flows, disbursements, and revenue streams.

The budget overlays the time and resource spreadsheets. The ultimate aim is a plan-driven budget, not a budget-driven plan.

Control Processes

Earned value analysis (also known as variance analysis) is a way to measure, evaluate, and control project performance. It compares the amount of work planned with what

Figure 7-12. Project Budget Spreadsheet.

Tasks	Month 1	Month 2	Month 3	Month 4	Month 5	Totals
WP-1						
Labor						
Labor OH						
Materials						
ODCs						
WP-2						
Labor						
Labor OH						
Materials						
ODCs						
Total						
CTD						

is actually accomplished to determine if the project is on track.

Planned value (PV) is the planned cost of work scheduled to be done in a given time period. The amount of PV is determined by adding the cost estimates for the activities scheduled to be completed in the time period. Planned value is also called the *budgeted cost of work scheduled (BCWS)*. This information is the base from which we later monitor progress, discern variances, and initiate corrective actions. Planned value answers the question "What did we think would happen by this date and how much did we think it would cost?"

Earned value (EV) is the planned cost of work actually

performed in a given time period. This is a measure of the dollar value of the work actually performed. The amount of EV is determined by adding the cost estimates for the activities that were actually completed in the time period. Earned value is also called the *budgeted cost of work performed (BCWP)*. Earned value answers the question "What really happened up to this point and how much did we think it was going to cost?"

Actual cost (AC) is the cost incurred to complete the work that was actually performed in a given time period. The amount of AC is determined by totaling the expenditures for the work performed in the given time period. Actual cost is also called the *actual cost of work performed (ACWP)*. Actual cost answers the question "What really happened up to this point and how much did it cost?"

Once these values are determined, you can use them in various combinations to provide measures of whether work is being accomplished as planned.

- *Schedule Variance (SV) = EV − PV.* This calculation measures the difference between the planned and the actual work completed. A positive result means the project is ahead of schedule; a negative result means the project is behind schedule.
- *Cost Variance (CV) = EV − AC*. This measures the difference between the planned (budgeted) cost and the actual cost of work completed. A positive result means the project is under budget; a negative result means the project is over budget.

Once these calculations are made, various indices or ratios can be used to evaluate the status and effectiveness of project work. These efficiency indicators provide valuable information that can be used to control the project. The two most commonly used are the *schedule performance index* and the *cost performance index.*

- *Schedule Performance Index (SPI) = EV / PV.* This ratio is a measure of efficiency in the schedule. A value less than one means the project has accomplished less than planned and is behind schedule; a value greater than one means the project is ahead of schedule.
- *Cost Performance Index (CPI) = EV / AC.* This ratio is a measure of cost efficiency (how efficiently dollars are being spent). A value less than one means the work is costing more than planned; a value greater than one means the work is being produced for less than planned. For example, a CPI of 0.67 means that for each dollar spent on the project, we produced $0.67 worth of value.

These items can be displayed in reports, spreadsheets, histograms, or graphs. Figure 7-13 is a graph showing cumulative costs in terms of the planned value. Figure 7-14 shows the difference in cumulative costs based on early, scheduled, and late start dates.

Organization Plan

The project's organization plan clarifies the relationship between departments (sometimes called the *organizational breakdown structure*) and the work items established in the work breakdown structure.

Figure 7-13. Cumulative Costs Based on Planned Value.

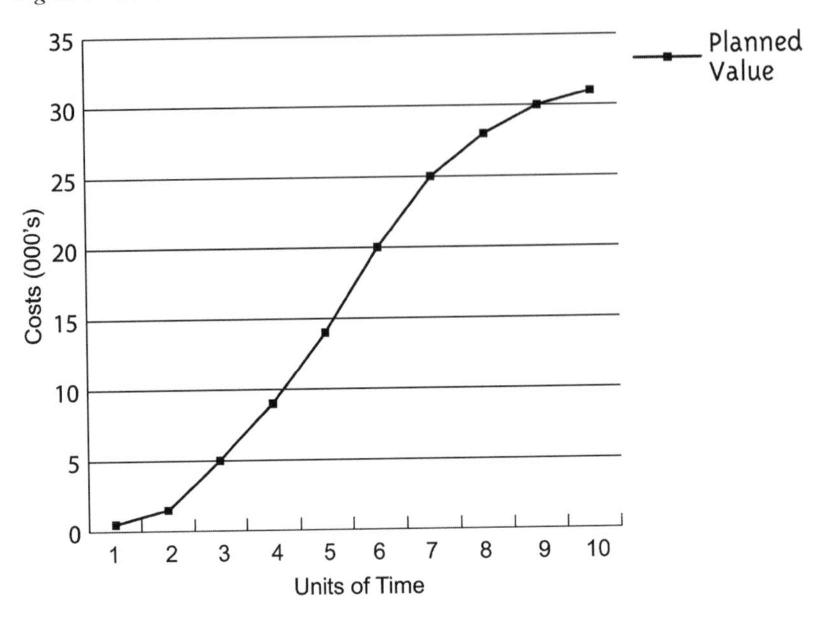

Once again, using the spreadsheet method, row entries define the work packages. Column headings define organizational units. These units may be within or external to the performing organization. This allows you to establish with care what outside vendors or third parties owe the project. In any case, the cells define the relationship that each organizational unit has in relationship to each work package. One scheme to define these relationships uses this nomenclature:

- A = directly performs the work; is answerable for the quality of the end item
- B = reviews work to determine adherence to quality standards

Figure 7-14. Cumulative Costs Based on Start Dates.

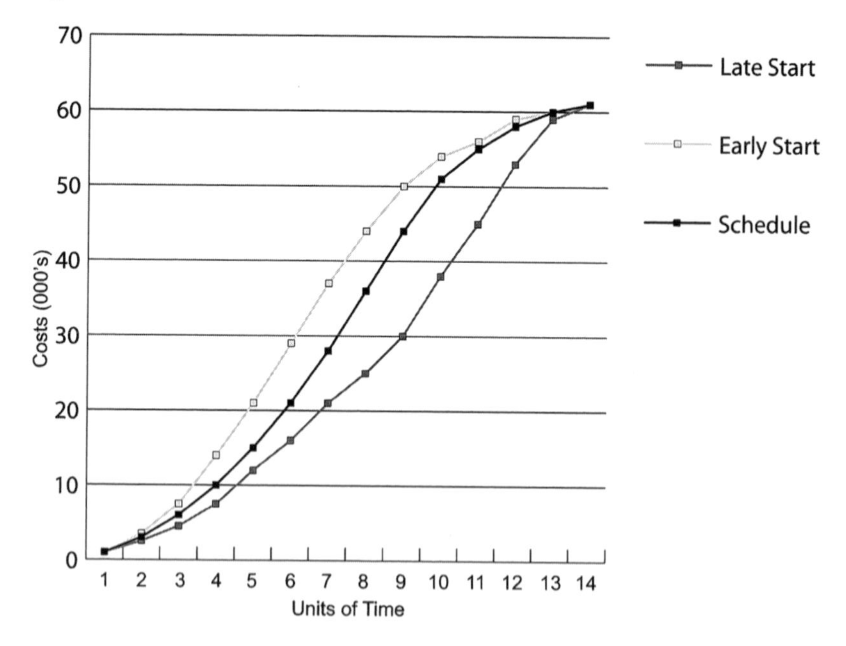

- C = has the authority to approve intermediate deliverables
- D = must be consulted prior to a decision; mandatory input
- E = may be consulted prior to a decision
- F = must be notified after a decision is made
- X = may exercise veto power regarding a specific work product
- O = may override the veto

Risk Management

Projects are investments and the project manager is responsible for achieving specific benefits within targets of time, cost, asset utilization, and resource utilization. However, every investment comes with risks. No one can predict with certainty the source, timing, significance, or impact of problems.

This book addressed project risk and project contingencies in Chapter 6. This section provides an overview of risk analysis as it applies to projects.

Risk management occurs throughout the life of a project, with increasing levels of detail at each succeeding phase. Whenever it occurs, the essential elements of a risk assessment are the following:

- ❑ Risk management planning
- ❑ Risk identification
- ❑ Qualitative risk analysis
- ❑ Quantitative risk analysis
- ❑ Risk response planning
- ❑ Risk monitoring and control

The first three elements can be summarized in a table that asks project team members to identify risks and then categorize them in two dimensions: likelihood (or probability of occurring) and the consequences (impacts). The results are used to populate the cells in the table shown in Figure 7-15.

After the risks have been named and measured, the next stages of risk management are to develop appropriate responses to the risk, then monitor and control the risk. These stages deal with:

- ❑ Prevention
- ❑ Detection
- ❑ Emergency responses and procedures
- ❑ Mitigation of loss or damage
- ❑ Detailed damage assessment
- ❑ Restoration and recovery

COMMUNICATION PLAN

The project manager should develop a communication plan for the project. A communication plan describes what information is communicated, to whom, how, and how often. You may wish to use a communication matrix like the one shown in Figure 7-16.

Figure 7-15. Risk Probability vs. Impact.

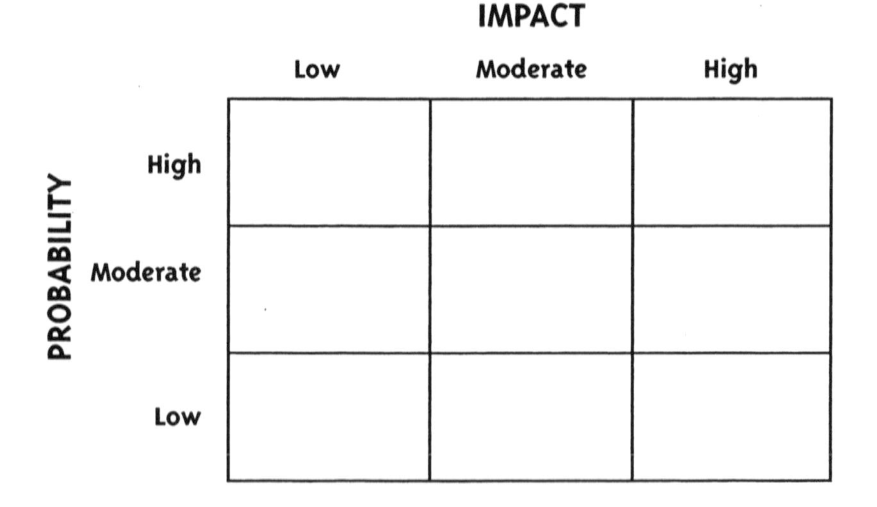

Figure 7-16. Communication Matrix.

What	Client	Customer	Team member A	Team member B
Formal status reports	monthly	quarterly	weekly	weekly
Phone calls and e-mail	as needed	as needed	as needed	as needed
Team meetings	minutes weekly	as needed	attends weekly	attends weekly
Status report on project website	daily	daily	daily	daily

Documentation and Commitments

The planning process ends with documentation and commitments to perform the work. The end result of the project planning process is not only a management plan, but also a political document. The plan is built as a collaborative effort. The project manager guides the planning team through a several step process. Throughout this process, the project manager orchestrates five critical interfaces:

1. *Formal Organizations:* defining their roles and responsibilities, authority, and accountability
2. *Material, Equipment, and Supplies:* coordinating from definition through solicitation, acquisition, deployment, use, and retirement
3. *Deliverables and Milestones:* acting as coach for a relay team, ensuring that a baton was passed seamlessly from one runner to the next

4. *Team Members:* serving as a leader through communicating, solving problems, and motivating
5. *Information Management:* ensuring that each stakeholder receives information that is accurate, timely, relevant, and concise

The planning process ends when the integrated plan obtains the authorization from senior management to proceed. In general, it is good practice to be sure the following events occur:

- ❑ The project manager and planning team members indicate their role in planning the project, indicate their willingness to serve as implementers of the plan, and convey their support of the plan.
- ❑ Resource managers (usually functional managers or department heads) indicate their approval of the plan and their commitment to provide specific resources to the project, in number, skill level, mix, timing, and place.
- ❑ Senior managers authorize performance of the work (along with approvals from customers, clients, and end users, as the case demands) and agree to provide the project manager and the team with the fiscal, physical, and intellectual resources needed for the project.

Part IV

PROJECT CONTROL

CHAPTER

–8–

Monitoring and Controlling Projects

Once approved, the integrated project plan becomes the basis for two closely related processes: execution and control. The central idea is that (1) work is authorized and performed according to the plan, (2) variances between plan and actual are detected promptly, (3) causes for the variance are identified, (4) alternative corrective actions are developed and assessed, (5) recommended corrective actions are approved and then implemented, and (6) plan documentation is updated to reflect the new reality. Control is designed to make reality conform to the plan and, where that is not possible, to make the new plan conform to reality.

Control tools include an approved baseline plan, current status information, completion estimates, current and future variances with impact assessment, alternative solutions with evaluation and recommendations, and approval from a change control board.

This chapter addresses ways to execute an approved project plan and control work in process, including the following:

- Determining the status of plan parameters
- Detecting current and future variances
- Preparing reports
- Developing alternative plans for corrective action
- Securing approvals
- Communicating revisions to the approved plans

Project Kickoff Meeting

Once you have an approved and completed integrated project plan published and distributed, it is time for you to arrange for the project sponsor to host a project kickoff meeting as a public display that communicates the importance of the project, the confidence of the sponsor in you and your plan, and the level of authority with which you have been entrusted. The sponsor should invite everyone (at all levels in all organizations) who has a vital interest in the conduct or outcome of the project.

Project Control

Project control, like the supervision of routine operations, is done in two ways: formally and informally. Figure 8-1

Figure 8-1. Types of Project Control.

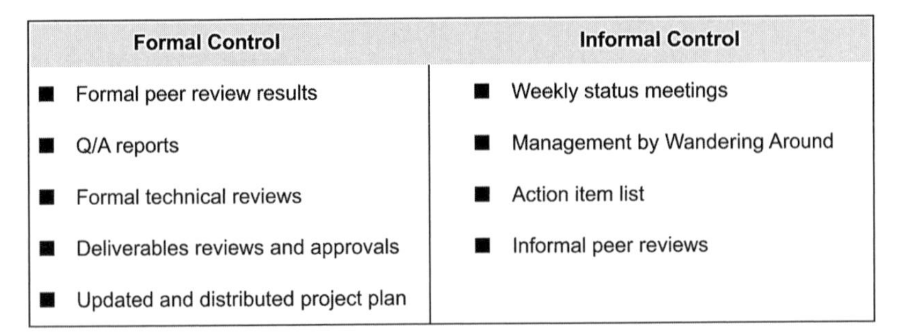

Formal Control	Informal Control
■ Formal peer review results	■ Weekly status meetings
■ Q/A reports	■ Management by Wandering Around
■ Formal technical reviews	■ Action item list
■ Deliverables reviews and approvals	■ Informal peer reviews
■ Updated and distributed project plan	

illustrates each approach. It is important to use both methods of control.

Project Meetings

An important part of project control is to conduct regular project meetings. Although project status information is gathered and reported outside of meetings, the regular project meetings provide a forum to discuss project issues and exceptions. Best practice is to schedule the meetings on a regular basis at a set time. Don't try to resolve all issues in these meetings. When serious project problems arise, schedule separate resolution meetings with the necessary participants.

Project Control Process

Figure 8-2 shows a typical control process, which has the following ten steps:

1. Determine the most recently approved version of the execution plan.

Figure 8-2. Project Control Process.

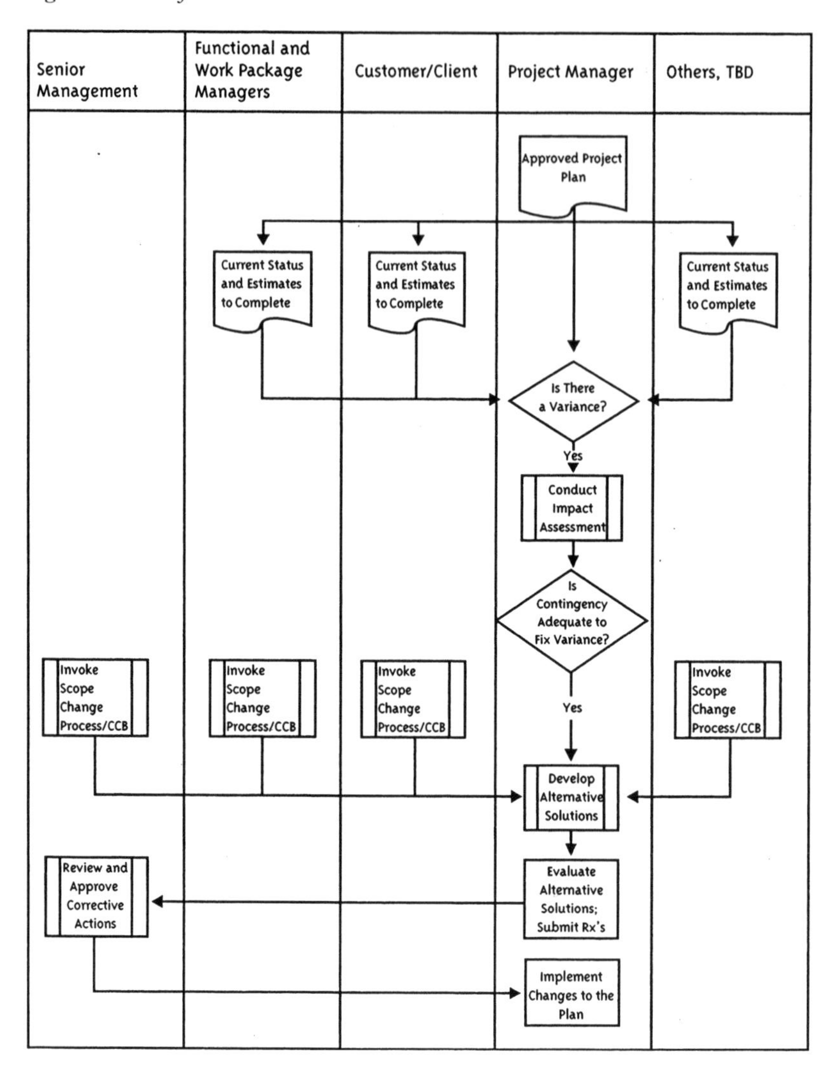

2. Collect current status information for open work packages.
3. Collect estimates-to-complete for open work packages.
4. Determine current and forecast variances from the plan.
5. Determine the impact of variances to decide if corrective action is required.
6. Identify corrective-action alternatives.
7. Select the preferred alternative.
8. Secure necessary approvals and authorizations.
9. Update the plan.
10. Publish and distribute the revised plan.

MONITORING PROJECT WORK

The approved project plan is the foundation for monitoring and tracking work in progress. The current baseline plan, plus information on current status, helps answer five crucial questions:

1. What work should be accomplished to date (in terms of time, resources, costs, and milestones)? That is, what is the project's planned condition?
2. What work has been accomplished to date? That is, what is the actual condition of the project?
3. Where is the project heading and when will it get there? That is, what is the forecast state of the project if we take no corrective actions?
4. What are the current and forecast variances in the project?
5. What, if anything, should be done?

Consider the following maxim: *The level at which you plan is the level at which you thereafter control!* If your work breakdown structure defines the project to three levels, you cannot monitor and control progress at any greater level of detail. If your project budget is merely a lump sum for each phase or stage, then you cannot capture cost information at the level of discrete work packages. The same holds true for labor hours, equipment, supplies, travel, and so on.

SCHEDULE IMPORTANCE

Schedule status becomes increasingly critical when time-to-market drives a project. This section of the chapter provides an extended example of how to track a project's schedule. Let us start with basic information about an engineering project. The goal of the project is to design and prepare for manufacturing a new product: a left-handed doodad.

The work packages have been defined, the dependency relationships are clear, and their estimated durations have been agreed. The result is shown in Figure 8-3.

The total project duration is expected to be fifty-five days and the plan is punctuated with two key milestones. Item five is a critical design review after three work packages have been done. Item ten is a preproduction meeting held after the prototype has been built, tested, and repaired.

The resulting schedule is displayed as a Gantt chart in Figure 8-4. To use this view for control purposes, you must save it as a *baseline*. This creates a fixed position from which to track work and detect variances. Regardless of which project management software you select, your plan will show at least two bars for each work package: planned and current status.

Figure 8-3. A Baseline Schedule Plan (Activity Sheet View).

ID	❶	Task Name	Duration	Start	Finish	Predecessors
1		**Project Doodad**	**55 days**	**Mon 10/8/01**	**Fri 12/21/01**	
2		Design Electrical	15 days	Mon 10/8/01	Fri 10/26/01	
3		Design Mechanical	15 days	Mon 10/8/01	Fri 10/26/01	
4		Design Hydraulic	15 days	Mon 10/8/01	Fri 10/26/01	
5		Critical Design Review	0 days	Fri 10/26/01	Fri 10/26/01	2,3,4
6		Build Prototype	10 days	Mon 10/29/01	Fri 11/9/01	5
7		Test Prototype	5 days	Mon 11/12/01	Fri 11/16/01	6
8		Document Exceptions	5 days	Mon 11/19/01	Fri 11/23/01	7
9		Repair Puchlist Items	10 days	Mon 11/26/01	Fri 12/7/01	8
10		Pre-Production Meeting	0 days	Fri 12/7/01	Fri 12/7/01	9
11		Scale-Up	10 days	Mon 12/10/01	Fri 12/21/01	10

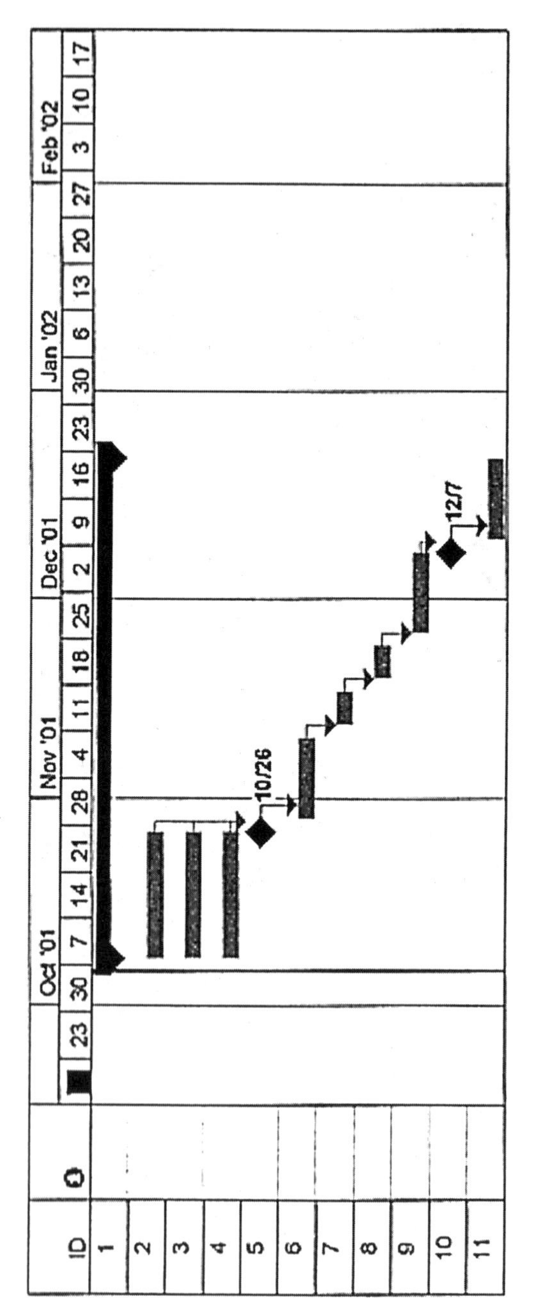

Figure 8-4. Project Schedule (Gantt Chart View).

Figure 8-5 shows the baseline schedule for our sample project.

We have decided to track progress on a weekly basis. In this example, we will track progress at the end of the second week. There are only three work packages that are open (on lines two, three, and four). We asked the activity managers, "How much more time do you need to complete your work?" Their responses were the following:

- ❑ Electrical engineering reported, "I need a week to finish my assigned activity."
- ❑ Mechanical engineering reported, "I'll be done in a few days."
- ❑ Hydraulic engineering reported, "I need two weeks from today to get finished."

The software display with this information may look like Figure 8-6.

The open space (at the left) of lines two, three, and four conveys work done; the solid bars show duration remaining for each activity. This figure tells us that all three of the design work packages should be completed at the same time. At two weeks into a three-week effort, each work package should have a two-week open bar and a one-week solid bar. Instead, it appears that work package one is on schedule, work package two is ahead of schedule, and work package three is behind schedule and will be a full week late in making its deliverable.

A related method of displaying schedule progress uses the percent complete of the activity. That view would appear as depicted in Figure 8-7 on page 166.

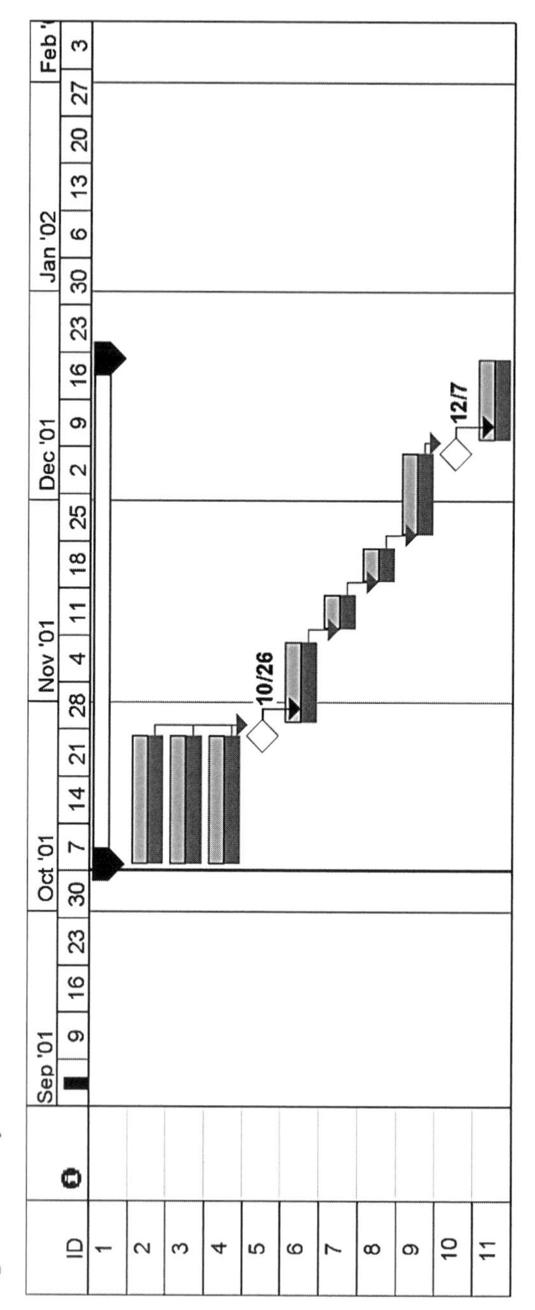

Figure 8-5. Project Baseline Schedule.

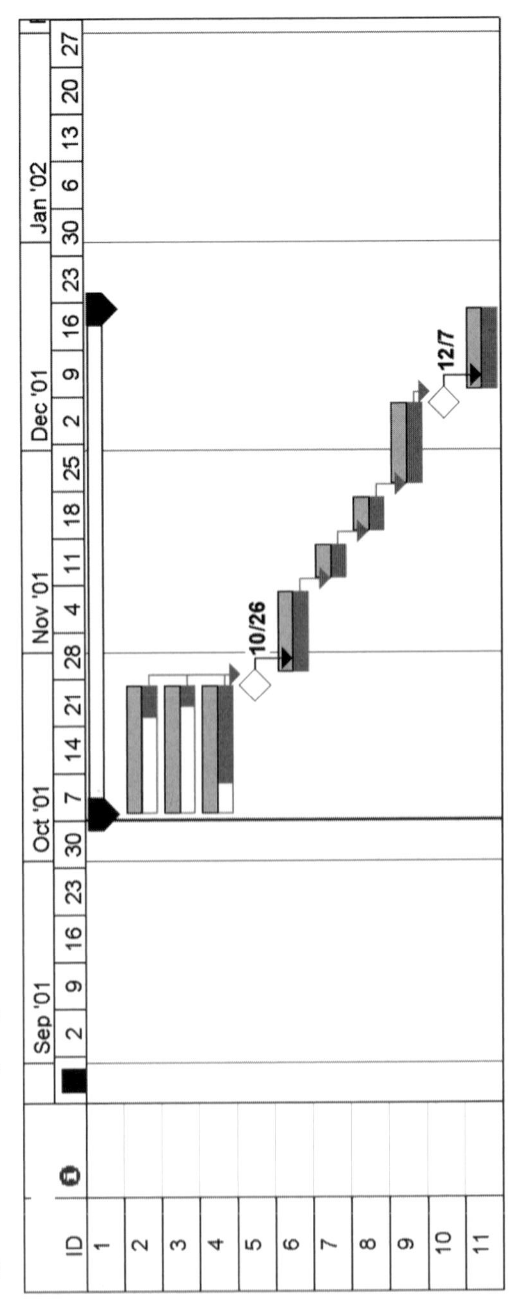

Figure 8-6. Status Report of Work in Process.

Figure 8-7. Schedule Status (Using Percent Complete).

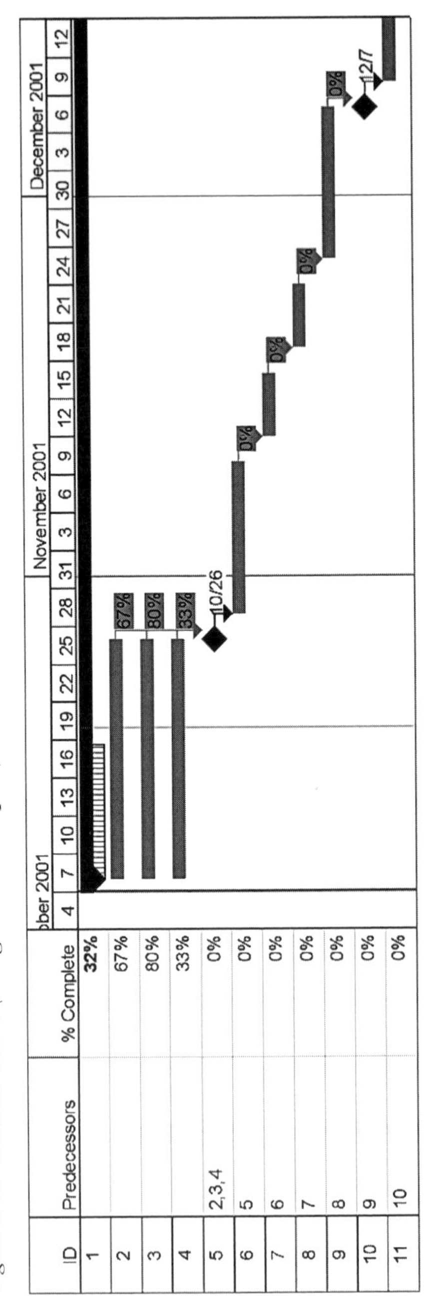

Knowing the status, however, is not enough. We need to understand the impact of the current status on the project's future. To do this, we assume that we do not use any corrective actions and that we do not change the dependency relationships among the activities. Figure 8-8 shows the results of this analysis.

- ❑ What will happen to the late finish date of the project?
- ❑ Is every activity still on the critical path?
- ❑ Which activities (suddenly) have float associated with them?

Labor Hours

Labor hours and cost reporting should follow the same general format. A sample report format appears in Figure 8-9.

For columns three to nine, the entries can be in labor hours (from a time tracking or labor distribution system) or in dollars (from an accounts payable, accrual, or commitment accounting system). This form is helpful with small or moderate-size projects. It would be cumbersome for larger projects. Therefore, it may be helpful to aggregate these data and display them as trend charts. A typical trend chart is shown in Figure 8-10.

Data Analysis

There is a strong temptation to believe reports from computerized systems. However, project data must be analyzed carefully, not merely taken at face value. The following checklist may be helpful:

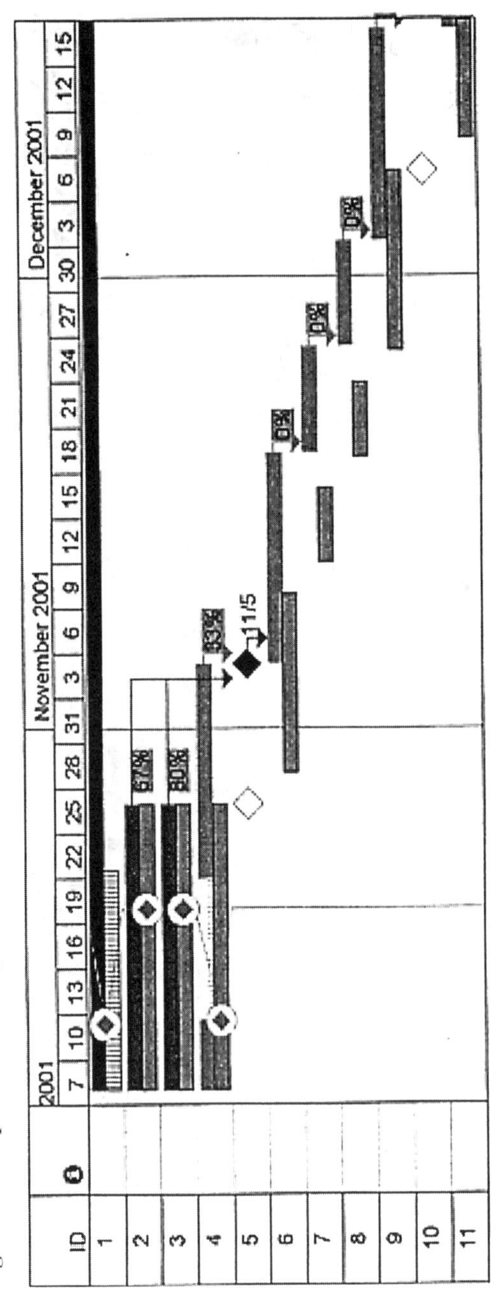

Figure 8-8. Impact Assessment of Schedule Variances (with No Corrective Actions).

Figure 8-9. Detailed Labor Hours Tracking Form.

1 WBS	2 Name	3 PTD	4 ATD	5 VTD	6 ETC	7 EAC	8 PAC	9 VAC
1.1								
1.2								
1.3								
1.4								
1.5								
1.6								
1.7								
1.8								
1.9								
1.10								
1.11								
Totals								
Source	Plan	Plan	LCR	(4-3)	WP Mgr	(4+6)	Plan	(8-7)

Figure 8-10. Project Trend Report.

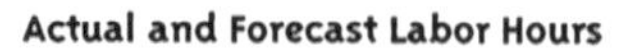

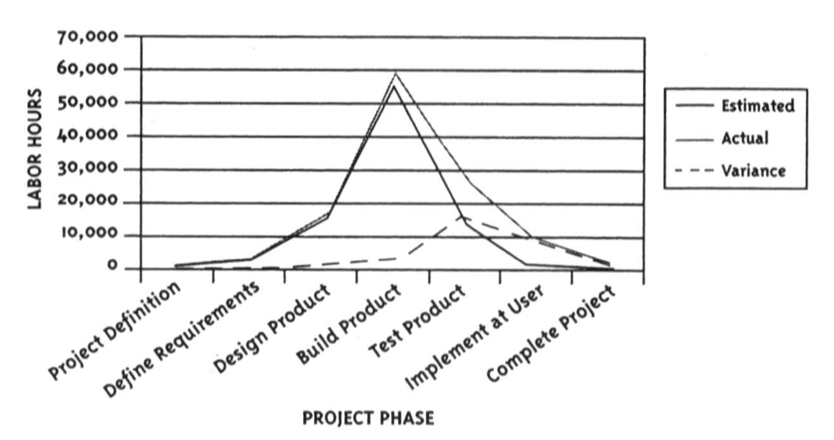

Sanity Check

- ❑ Does the report make sense?
- ❑ Is it plausible, timely, relevant, and complete?
- ❑ Does it show both breakdowns and breakthroughs?
- ❑ Are there any surprises? Does it match your experience?

Significance Test

- ❑ Are the variances trivial or significant?
- ❑ Are they offsetting or reinforcing?

Corrective Actions

- ❑ Does the report itself suggest corrective actions?
- ❑ Do the suggestions comply with project drivers?
- ❑ Schedule-driven projects may require additional costs.
- ❑ Budget-driven projects may require rescheduling.
- ❑ Requirements-driven projects may require both time and cost adjustments.
- ❑ Resource-constrained projects may require rescheduling.
- ❑ Any project may require the expenditure of contingency.
- ❑ Corrective actions require collaborative effort, much like the original planning process.

Change Control

Change is the constant in a project manager's life. As a practical matter, you must serve as gatekeeper for the change control process. The basic rule holds that no one can unilaterally change the scope of the project. All proposed scope changes must initially pass through the project manager. At this early stage, you may choose to:

- Agree to process the request (without guaranteeing the result or outcome)
- Defer processing of the change (usually because it comes at an inopportune time)
- Deny processing the request (because its consequences are negative and evident)

The steps that compose change management are as follows:

- Determine the current version of the execution plan.
- Receive the change request.
- Enter and update a change control log or journal.
- Determine (in your role as gatekeeper) whether to process the request.
- Assess the impact of the proposed change on the following:
  - Schedule
  - Costs
  - Asset usage
  - Resource usage
  - Exposure (or risk)
  - Effect on other project or nonproject work

- ❑ Prepare recommendations.
- ❑ Submit recommendations to the change control board.
- ❑ Obtain approvals.
- ❑ Update project plans.
- ❑ Distribute updated plans.
- ❑ Monitor and track against the revised plan.

Sources of Change

Changes to project scope may come from several sources. Try to anticipate changes from the following sources or reasons:

- ❑ *Structure:* organizational changes rearrange reporting relationships and hierarchies
- ❑ *Staffing:* people change positions or assume new roles and responsibilities
- ❑ *Strategy:* business priorities change in response to market forces, mergers, acquisitions, and divestitures
- ❑ *Systems:* technology influences the choice of configurations and business processes
- ❑ *Public Policy:* changes caused by elections, statutes, or regulations
- ❑ *Design Reviews:* customer or end user initiates changes based on intermediate deliverables or test results

Regardless of the source, project changes have two consequences:

1. If the project's overall scope changes, then the underlying plan must also change. This requires some form of version control or configuration management process.
2. If the plan changes because you use part of the contingency or management reserve, then you must update the execution plan. This still leaves intact the project's targets for technical quality, a late finish date, and a ceiling on expenditures.

CHAPTER

–9–

CLOSING A PROJECT

Chapter 8 presented the processes, tools, and techniques that guide execution and control of a project. Project closure usually begins after the client has accepted the majority of the project deliverables. Sometimes a project will end prematurely or unsuccessfully. In either case, the project manager and team must obtain closure before moving on to their next assignment. Additionally, the team, client, and stakeholders will be concerned both about the disposition of this project and their immediate future. The following situations are common:

- Team members are concerned about their next assignment.

- The client or user organization is concerned about loss of technical competence and operational skill when you leave the project.
- Management wants you to start the next project immediately.
- Functional managers are curious about how their people performed.
- Everyone wants to know what lessons can be learned from this experience.

In this chapter we will review the needs of the client, stakeholders, and team members regarding project closure. We will discuss the steps necessary for completing project closure and describe techniques to enact those steps. Project closure is an important step that is often overlooked or poorly executed.

Benefits of Project Closure

There are many benefits associated with project closure. One key benefit is to ensure that you have met expectations and another is to gather and document lessons learned so you can incorporate successes and avoid problems in future work.

A formal acceptance by the client ensures that the project is truly finished and helps give finality to the project. This can minimize continuing calls from the client regarding product usage, bugs, or other questions, and it helps the team obtain closure and move on to other work with minimal disruption from the previous project.

Additional objectives of project closure include:

- ❑ Communicating staff performance
- ❑ Closing out all financial reports
- ❑ Improving estimates for future projects
- ❑ Improving project methodologies
- ❑ Smoothing the release of staff
- ❑ Ensuring client and stakeholder satisfaction

Project Closure Ensures Project Requirements Are Met

In Chapter 3, we discussed the concept of project scope. Project scope can be viewed from several perspectives and levels of detail. Using the goal breakdown structure also discussed in Chapter 3, the project manager defines the levels of detail as shown in Figure 9-1.

The project manager is ultimately responsible and accountable for the project requirements (level two). Classically, project closure is defined as meeting (or, in some cases, exceeding) requirements. A project is deemed complete and successful, at least for the project manager, when all requirements have been completed. This concept enforces the importance of measurable and verifiable require-

Figure 9-1. Goal Breakdown Structure (Reiterated).

Level	Definition
0	Project Goal (or Mission)
1	Project Objectives (Critical Success Factors)
2	Project Requirements (Critical Success Measures)
3	Specifications

ments. Increasingly, client organizations require the project team to prove each and every requirement before final payment is made. Proof can be provided in various ways, such as the following:

- Testing
- Analysis
- Inspection
- Interpolation

The precise measures and methods used will depend on the project's context. Sometimes, proof of completion relies on physical or chemical testing. For other projects, we conduct accelerated life-cycle testing, simulate or model a system's performance, or construct working prototypes. Occasionally, government rules dictate what constitutes completion and success. The essential point is that early definition of critical success factors and critical success measures gives us the project's *exit criteria*, helps to discipline the client's expectations, and helps control changes to project objectives.

Sometimes, a project manager will be faced with ill-defined requirements or client apathy regarding requirements. A plant manager might say, "I don't care how you do it, just reduce the failure rate of the widget line by 50 percent!" Here, the project manager still creates requirements, but closure cannot occur until the project objective has been met. This, of course, does not alleviate the project team from completing as-built documentation, training of the line workers, financial closure, or other means. Under these conditions, you must recognize that you are taking the role of the client and ensuring that the requirements will ultimately achieve the project objective.

Not all projects end with successful objectives or requirements. Many end prematurely, as described in Figure 9-2.

In these scenarios, the project team no longer needs to deliver product or services to the client (see Figure 9-3). However, this does not lessen the need for the project manager to conduct other project closure items as discussed throughout this chapter.

PROJECTS MAY END IN A VARIETY OF WAYS

All projects, by definition, must come to an end. How they get there will vary. In the book *Project Management: A Managerial Approach*, Jack R. Meredith and Samuel J. Mantel, Jr.

Figure 9-2. Reasons for Premature Project Closure.

Scenario	***Description***	***Detection and Prevention***
Project runs out of money or time, i.e., "starvation"	Cost and schedule are two legs of the project triangle.	Following proper project management methods, schedule and cost overruns should be highly anticipated. Project phase reviews are specifically designed to detect overruns and allow the project to shutdown in an orderly fashion.
Project no longer needed	Changes within the client's organization result in loss of demand for the project.	This can occur suddenly or expectedly.
Political battle	An organization member (on either the client or performing team side) kills the project through political means.	Project management methodologies are designed to both prevent and detect project politics.
Catastrophic events	This includes such items as the client filing bankruptcy, sale of the company, etc.	Such events occur without warning.

Figure 9-3. Process for Premature Project Closure.

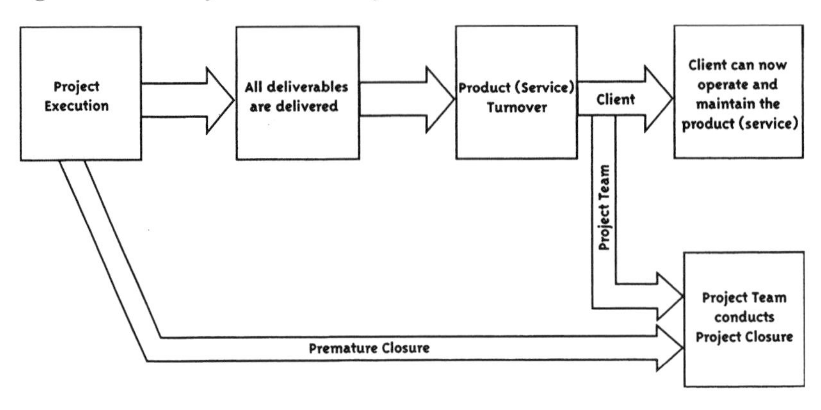

offer four useful categories to describe various project endings:

1. *Termination by Integration.* This is the most common and most complex type. All the assets and resources used in a project are redistributed among the existing elements of the organization. The output of the project becomes a standard part of operating systems and procedures. Transitional elements typically include the following business functions:
   - ❑ Personnel and human resources
   - ❑ Manufacturing, assembly, fabrication
   - ❑ Engineering
   - ❑ Accounting and finance
   - ❑ Purchasing and procurement
   - ❑ Legal, regulatory affairs, general counsel
   - ❑ Information systems and technology
   - ❑ Marketing and sales

- ❑ Distribution
- ❑ Customer service

2. *Termination by Starvation.* The project ends because the money runs out. In reality, this is not termination at all.
3. *Termination by Addition.* This is what happens when a project ends successfully and then migrates into the enterprise as a new business unit or product line. Project assets and resources migrate from the completed project to the new product business or division. In some companies, a deliberate career path is found as project managers successfully complete their work and become product managers.
4. *Termination by Extinction.* These are projects brought to an end (often before completion) because they are unsuccessful, fail to meet end-user objectives, are superseded by technical advances that make the project obsolete, or because cost escalations destroy economic viability of the project or product. In this case, technical work on the project may be suspended, but administrative work and organizational arrangements must be made to dispose of the project itself. Checklists must be completed, a final report drafted, lessons learned disseminated throughout the organization, and key staff must be assigned to new work efforts.

Closure Begins with Customer Acceptance

Informal project closure usually begins just as the client accepts the major deliverables. In most projects, the presentation of additional deliverables follows this step. These include such items as training, handholding, completing the as-built documentation, and other deliverables.

One of the first steps in initiating project closure is to contact the team members' resource managers to prepare them for the closure. This includes two important actions: (1) the managers need to determine the team members' next assignments and (2) the project manager needs to communicate staff-member performance to the resource managers. It is important to begin this step early. First, it may take time for the resource managers to plan the team members' actions and second, the staff may become concerned about their next assignments.

The project manager should meet with the team to review project closure issues such as the following:

- ❑ The team's new assignments
- ❑ Plans for lessons learned
- ❑ Assurance that all deliverables are presented and accepted
- ❑ Closure of administrative and financial information

The steps required for project closure are summarized in the checklist in Figure 9-4 at the end of this chapter (see page 186).

Lessons Learned

We discussed earlier in this chapter that one of the benefits of project closure is the provision of a methodology to prevent repeating mistakes. This includes identifying what went well and poorly during the project, documenting it, and communicating this information to everyone who may benefit from it. The following are sources for identifying lessons learned:

- *Change Log and Associated Change Management Forms.* The change logs and change management forms are excellent tools for developing improvement plans. Each change is a result of an alteration to the plan. If there were no project changes, all projects would be on time, on budget, and all goals would be met. The change management system, therefore, provides a history of all areas where project teams, stakeholders, project managers, senior management, and clients can improve.
- *Project Reviews During and at the Conclusion of the Project.* This may include interviews, questionnaires, or other formal and informal reviews with the project team, client, and stakeholders, which can also yield excellent ideas.
- *Written Notes Made During the Project.* Frequently, during a project someone will recognize a way to improve the process. This occurs frequently during problem-solving meetings. Someone will say, for example, "If we had interviewed the procurement manager, this never would have happened!" Experienced project managers will write these comments down and place them in a special section of the project book.

Once these improvement opportunities are identified, it is imperative that they be communicated to everyone who may benefit from them. If the organization has a defined methodology, the project manager formulates a final report that includes both project successes and ideas for methodology adjustments. The methodology owners gather this information and make appropriate changes. For other organizations, the project manager may simply document these ideas and disseminate them through status meetings with colleagues or through e-mail.

Finance and Administration Records

After the major deliverables are completed, the project manager and team accumulate final sets of actual data for the project. These include costs, work, and final product documentation. Ensure that final, actual data on activities are recorded. This information is useful for estimating future projects. Capture the final project costs and other financial information. Complete the financial reports required by your organization and submit them for approval. Ensure this step is done early enough to allow time for the finance group to provide feedback and handle requests for changes.

Finally, archive all information in your organization's formal archive.

Performance Reporting

This action is needed for all staff members who have spent a large amount of time on the project and don't report directly to you. When team members have worked on a project for an extended period, their direct managers may not have appropriate insight into their performance, making it difficult to establish appropriate raises, promotions, or demotions. To solve this issue, the project manager presents reports to these managers regarding performance. This also offers the project manager more authority. When team members know that you are going to report their performance to their manager, they will be motivated to perform better.

Staff Release

One of the final steps in closing a project is to release the remaining staff. This step should be planned early and communicated to the staff members to relieve their concerns for the future. One technique that may be employed for larger projects is to make the dismissal formal, either through a brief meeting where the project manager thanks the team or through a team celebration. This provides the team with final closure and allows them to proceed to their next assignments without lingering concerns.

At the outset, the project creates the team. At closure, the team created the project!

Figure 9-4. Project Closure Checklist.

Item	Responsibility	Due Date Scheduled	Due Date Actual
Project			
Have all activities in the project plan been completed?			
Have all work orders been completed?			
Have all contracts been completed?			
Have all outstanding commitments been resolved?			
Has the client or customer accepted the final products?			
Are all deliverables completed?			
Has agreement been reached with the client on the disposition of any remaining deliverables?			
Have external certifications and authorizations been signed and approved?			
Have all audits been completed and issues resolved?			
Have ongoing maintenance procedures been activated?			
Finances			
Have all payments been made to vendors and contractors?			
Have all costs been charged to the project?			
Have project accounts been closed?			
Have remaining project funds been returned?			
Project documentation			
Have project plans and supporting documentation been revised to reflect the "as-built" condition?			
Have final project reports been prepared and distributed?			
Has the project plan been archived with supporting data?			
Have "lessons learned" been documented, shared with appropriate people, and archived with the project plans?			
Personnel			
Are all parties aware of the pending closeout?			
Has effort been recognized and rewarded?			
Have project personnel been reassigned?			
Resources			
Has excess project material been dealt with?			
Have project facilities, equipment, and other resources been reallocated?			

APPENDIXES

Appendix A: Recommended Reading

Baker, Sunny, and Kim Baker. *The Complete Idiot's Guide to Project Management*. 2nd ed. Indianapolis: Alpha Books, 2000.

Boar, Bernard H. *The Art of Strategic Planning for Information Technology*. 2nd ed. New York: Wiley, 2001.

Cleland, David I., and Lewis R. Ireland. *Project Manager's Portable Handbook*. New York: McGraw Hill, 2000.

Gundry, Lisa, and Laurie LaMantia. *Breakthrough Teams for Breakneck Times*. Chicago: Dearborn Trade, 2001.

Hallows, Jolyon E. *Information Systems Project Management: How to Deliver Function and Value in Information Technology*. 2nd ed. New York: AMACOM, 2005.

Hooks, Ivy F., and Farry, Kristin A. *Customer-Centered Products*. New York: AMACOM, 2001.

Howes, Norman R. *Modern Project Management: Successfully Integrating Project Management Knowledge Areas and Processes*. New York: AMACOM, 2001.

Kerzner, Harold. *Project Management: A Systems Approach to Planning, Scheduling, and Controlling*. 8th ed. Hoboken, NJ: Wiley, 2003.

Kerzner, Harold. *In Search of Excellence in Project Management: Success Practices in High Performance Organizations*. New York: Van Nostrand Reinhold, 1998.

Lewis, James P. *Fundamentals of Project Management*, 2nd ed. New York: AMACOM, 2002.

Meredith, Jack R. and Samuel J. Mantel, Jr. *Project Management: A Managerial Approach*, 4th ed. New York: Wiley, 2000.

Newell, Michael W. *Preparing for the Project Management Professional (PMP®) Certification Exam*, 3rd ed. New York: AMACOM, 2005.

Pinto, Jeffrey K., ed. *The Project Management Institute: Project Management Handbook*. 1st ed. San Francisco: Jossey-Bass Publishers, 1998.

Project Management Institute. *A Guide to the Project Management Body of Knowledge (PMBOK® Guide)*. 3rd ed. Newtown Square, PA: Project Management Institute, 2004.

Project Management Institute. *Project Management Institute Practice Standard for Work Breakdown Structures.* Newtown Square, PA: Project Management Institute, 2001.

Richman, Larry. *Project Management Step-by-Step.* New York: AMACOM, 2002.

Thomsett, Michael C. *The Little Black Book of Project Management.* 2nd ed. New York: AMACOM, 2002.

Wysocki, Robert K. *Building Effective Project Teams.* New York: Wiley, 2002.

Appendix B: Templates for the Project Plan

Critical Path Bar Chart Template

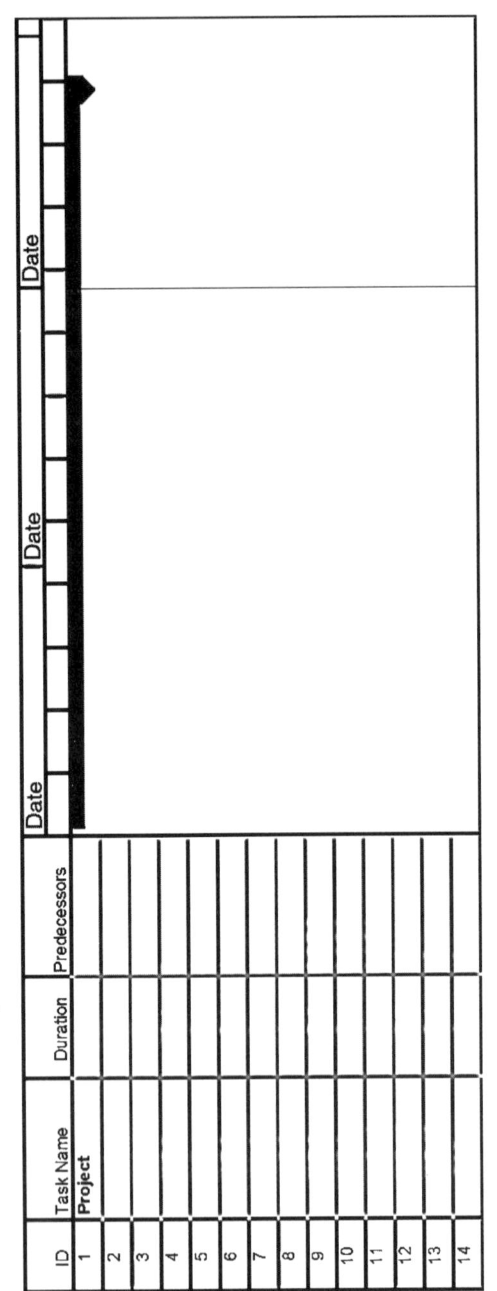

Project Work Breakdown Structure (with Durations and Dependencies) Template

ID		Duration	Predecessors
1			
2			
3			
4			
5			
6			
7			
8			
9			
10			
11			
12			
13			
14			
15			
16			
17			
18			
19			
20			
21			
22			
23			
24			
25			
26			
27			
28			
29			
30			
31			
32			
33			
34			
35			
36			
37			
38			
39			
40			
41			
42			
43			
44			
45			
46			
47			
48			
49			
50			
51			
52			
53			
54			
55			
56			
57			
58			
59			

Template for Planning Steps for Resource Planning and Budgeting

Who	Does What	Product

Enterprise Skills Inventory Template

Staff	R&D	EE	Arch	Hydro	Nuclear	Inst

Resource Table Template

ID	❶	Resource Name	Initials	Group	Max. Units	Std. Rate	Ovt. Rate	Cost/Use
1								
2								
3								
4								
5								
6								
7								
8								
9								
10								

Resources Assigned to Work Packages Template

ID	Resource Names	Task Name	Duration	Predecessors
1				
2				
3				
4				
5				
6				
7				
8				
9				
10				
11				
12				
13				
14				
15				
16				
17				
18				
19				
20				
21				
22				

Index